Simply Delishaas

Simply Delishaas

favorite recipes from my midwestern kitchen

Hayden Haas

Publisher Mike Sanders
Art & Design Director William Thomas
Editorial Director Ann Barton
Senior Editor Molly Ahuja
Designer Lindsay Dobbs
Photographer Tessa Hiney
Production Manager Melina Moser
Food Stylist Casey Gipson
Food Styling Assistant Daniel Isaacson
Food Styling Assistant Corren Leech
Prop Stylist Haley Lukaczyk
Proofreader Claire Safran
Indexer Beverlee Day

First American Edition, 2024
Published in the United States by DK Publishing
1745 Broadway, 20th Floor, New York, NY 10019

The authorized representative in the EEA is Dorling Kindersley
Verlag GmbH. Arnulfstr. 124, 80636 Munich, Germany

A catalog record for this book
is available from the Library of Congress.
ISBN 978-0-7440-8965-3

DK books are available at special discounts when purchased
in bulk for sales promotions, premiums, fund-raising, or
educational use. For details, contact SpecialSales@dk.com

Printed and bound in China

www.dk.com

MIX
Paper | Supporting
responsible forestry
FSC™ C018179

This book was made with Forest
Stewardship Council™ certified
paper – one small step in DK's
commitment to a sustainable future.
Learn more at
www.dk.com/uk/information/sustainability

About the Author

Hayden Haas is a recipe developer, food photographer, and food stylist. He's also the funny and handsome digital content creator behind the satirical, unscripted video blog @Delishaas. Hayden launched his online platform in the fall of 2020 and has been sharing his midwestern-inspired creations ever since. Hayden (and his recipes) have appeared on Food Network's *Chopped*, *Girl Meets Farm*, and *Good Morning America*. He has also partnered with *Bon Appétit*, and Target. Hayden lives in Grand Forks, North Dakota, with his canine companion and kitchen assistant, Max.

This book is dedicated to my chosen family.

FOREWORD

When the world took an awful turn in March 2020, Hayden entered my life like the warm ray of sunshine that he is, lighting my way through that very dark time. My show had just shut down filming mid-episode and as the film crew flew home for an indefinite amount of time, and I wondered what on earth the next few months would look like with a looming book deadline and new baby, Hayden swooped in with the exact words I needed to hear: I can help! And now years later I can say that "help" doesn't even begin to describe the difference he made in my life. Because it wasn't just about the countless deli containers of recipes that he'd diligently prepped and tested and dropped off at my door, it was also about the sense of care that he brought with it and the feelings of positivity and encouragement that he exuded during every interaction with him. Hayden is programmed to nurture those around him, like the biggest warmest hug imaginable, and to make you feel like with whatever recipe attempt you've just failed at or whatever bad day you've had, it will all be okay. And isn't that exactly how you want to feel when you're sitting down to a hot, home-cooked meal?

As he helped me with my recipes I also watched from a so-close-yet-so-far distance as he began creating his own recipes and going viral with them (and then delivering those recipes for me to gobble). He introduced me to Korean corn dogs, his famous cranberry sauce, and cheeseburger soup, and kept me in the loop about all of the tastiness going viral in his corner of the internet, like that dangerous baked feta pasta. What was so thrilling about Hayden's success wasn't just the happiness that I could see on his face every time he came up with a new crazy recipe idea or reached a new tier of TikTok followers, it was that I knew this newfound reach was helping to spread his joy around the world. Suddenly so many people were experiencing the things I got to see first hand: his infectious positivity, his ability to welcome absolutely everybody to his table, and of course, his unabashed enthusiasm for food. And really delicious, comforting, hearty food at that.

What I'm getting at is: the world needs more Haydens. His jolly, warm, excitable energy makes everything taste delicious and it gives everybody around him a little pep in their step. So until cloning is a real thing and we can all have a Hayden living down the street to brighten up our days, we have this book and it's with this book that you and your kitchen will gain a little bit of that Hayden spark in your life.

Enjoy,
Molly Yeh

CONTENTS

Brekkie, Drag Brunch & Lunch

Breakfast & Brunch

Appetizers & Finger Foods

Handhelds

Cravings for Occasions & IRL (In Real Life)

The Meat & Potatoes of Things

Oh, the Pasta-bilities

Casseroles, Hot Dishes & Other Midwest-y Stuff

INTRODUCTION

Hi there! My name is Hayden Haas, and I am a food blogger and recipe developer at @Delishaas. I was born and raised in North Dakota's Red River Valley, a wonderfully fertile part of the world known for its farms and fields of sugar beets, potatoes, golden wheat, sunflowers, and corn. I began my adventure in the culinary world as a food-loving kid. My appreciation of food and Midwestern-inspired cooking has deep-buried roots in church picnics and basement potlucks and long, cold winters spent gathered around a warm fireplace. I am inspired by my parents, friends, and other family members who instilled in me the joy of food, its power to bring people together, and the importance of celebrating the simple things in life. I owe so much to the women of my family: my mom and my grandmothers. (Who runs the world? Girls!) I'm grateful to my mom especially, for introducing such a variety of cultures and foods into our family meals as I was growing up.

My childhood summers mostly were spent in northern Wisconsin at my Grandma Geneva's cabin on the lake. A short ride down the road was my Grandma Mary's family-owned butcher shop and and general store. We often gathered at the kitchen table or fire pit while camping, and we always had plenty of wonderful food to go around.

I show love—like many of you—by sitting down, breaking bread, and having a meal with someone. To be able to nourish another person is a wonderful thing, whether you're making someone you love a bowl of pasta on a Tuesday night, baking a special cake for a birthday, or creating a spectacular wedding cake. Cooking takes time, effort, money, and, perhaps the most important and cost-effective ingredient, LOVE. (Or at least that's what my grandmothers would say, and now I know it to be true.)

Before we get too far, I want to say that originally I was going to make a drinking game for all the dumb wisecracks I write in this book, but for your liver's safety, and to prevent skyrocketing alcohol sales in liquor stores everywhere, I have decided against doing that. Still, you've been warned! (I do hope you'll chuckle a bit throughout though.)

In 2017, I graduated college with a degree in architectural drafting and interior design. (And was voted the best smile and class clown—honors I cherish!) My studies helped me learn how to write instructions more clearly and taught me how to

properly assemble things, like a residential house, which is knowledge I now use to assemble cakes! I never imagined that my degree would help me with my work in the food business, but it has been a very useful foundation for building @Delishaas.

An important part of my cooking journey has been learning how to share and love my true self. Coming out as gay was a life-affirming event for me. I know what you're going to say: "What does your cooking journey have to do with your sexuality?" Nothing really, but it was the beginning of my own road to self-acceptance and a commitment to living authentically. I'm not going to sugarcoat it: I was quite depressed and struggled for a long time with the fear that I would never find happiness. But, although life still has its challenges, my sense of belonging, acceptance, and community has lifted me in ways I never would have imagined. When I started @Delishaas, I made the commitment to share my love of great food with anyone who wanted to help me make the world a better place.

If I hadn't put in the work and gone through the steps to accept my genuine self, I wouldn't have been able to write this book. The fear of what others might think, or backlash, is real, and it took me all of 27 years to work through that fear. (That's a lot of time wasted not being happy!) I don't want to sound like a congressman with a false sense of altruism—the Swifties will know what I mean—it's just love.

This brings us to 2019, when I found myself working as a manager at a very popular retailer in Grand Forks, North Dakota. (You might recognize it from its red and white bull's-eye logo.) When I wasn't working, you could find me in my kitchen, creating new recipes or preparing for an upcoming brunch I was hosting. This might sound strange, but I had not been using any social media platforms since high school (because I was in the closet and jealous of everyone else living a happy life). After the longest time of living somewhat disingenuously, I decided to focus on my love of cooking and my newly found interest in food photography. As a result, @Delishaas was born!

Meanwhile, I had just found out that a Food Network star lived in my very own small town... like, what?! I could sense that opportunity was cooking up something sweet for me.

Introducing Molly Yeh, the Sprinkle Queen herself, host of *Girl Meets Farm* on Food Network, and blogger from My Name Is Yeh. Miraculously, Molly had just posted a position for a culinary assistant, so of course I had to apply! After sending in my application, I learned the position had already been filled, but I must have made a good impression because Molly reached out and asked me if I'd be interested in working with the production company on her television show. I later found out that the job primarily required washing dishes (among a million other cool hats you wear in that position!).

Even though my dislike of dishwashing is well known among my friends and family, I said yes to this once-in-a-lifetime opportunity. It was, in fact, great. I had so much fun meeting so many amazing people who worked diligently behind the scenes, and Molly and her family are wonderful people. After working on the television set for about two months, I decided to take a job as a freelance film production assistant (the bottom of the food chain). Of course, then the pandemic hit. To put it politely, I was royally fucked (like a lot of people were).

Luckily for me, Molly's previous assistant had moved out of town about that time, while Molly was writing her book, *Home Is Where the Eggs Are*. She asked if I was still interested in the position, and of course I said, "YES, I'm happy to help!" While working with Molly and her team, I learned so much about recipe development, food styling, and all the magic that happens behind the scenes. Using the skills I developed on set, I began sharing my knowledge on TikTok and Instagram, posting recipes for some of my favorite Midwest-inspired foods. @Delishaas was quickly turning into a full-time job—one that I didn't know how to explain to my parents! The internet is crazy, y'all.

I'm constantly being asked, "Do you actually make money from your work?" The short answer is yes, but it's hard to describe my job because it's not very common and it's constantly evolving. I usually say, "I would be posting the things I do regardless of whether I had a following or not because I enjoy it and it makes people happy." I don't really feel comfortable being called an influencer, but I do appreciate the responsibilities and power of the social media medium to share and influence. I will always insist that the only thing I'd like to influence you to do is to spread kindness and share wonderful food. So, like most other people when the pandemic happened, I took to the internet and made silly videos on TikTok. To my shock, my platform grew and grew. If you are one of my followers, THANK YOU, again. I am brought to tears every day because I'm so thankful for you and the community that is behind @Delishaas. Pinch me because this doesn't feel real.

This brings us to the here and now. In this cookbook, you'll find my favorite creations. Each recipe brings a sense of nostalgia, community, and inclusivity along with amazing flavors. As a member of the LBGTQIA+ community and a human of the world, I'm committed to sharing my belief in the power of food to bring people together. I'm also excited to share my passion for cooking... and a bunch of dumb but occasionally witty and sometimes hilarious jokes all tied together with anecdotes and stories. I guarantee it will be an enjoyable and delicious read. Bon appétit!

ESSENTIAL KITCHEN TOOLS

"You can buy the tools you need with thyme."—Shakespeare (if he was a cook)

This section is devoted to my favorite kitchen tools that I believe are worthy of precious counter and drawer space.

Stand mixer: I think anyone who enjoys baking would say that a quality stand mixer is a vital tool, not only because it saves you time (and arm strength!), but also because it can be used in so many ways: mixing batters, beating frosting, churning ice cream, prepping pasta dough, and even shredding roasted chicken. A stand mixer also is handy when you're trying to throw something together and you're maxing out your multitasking skills; you can set it up, walk away from it, and allow it to continue working while you prep another task. It's the handiest kitchen appliance, second only perhaps to a fridge or a stove, but worth every penny.

These can be a little spendy, TBH. When I received my first stand mixer as a gift at 25 years old, it felt as if I had just gotten married to myself. Friends were constantly receiving them as wedding gifts, and I was so jealous—and so painfully single—so it meant that much more when I finally got my hands on one. (Not to mention that my forearms were more than ready for a break!)

Food processor: A good food processor—and by good, I mean big—is another time-saving kitchen essential. Bigger isn't always better when it comes to kitchen appliances, but in this case, it is. I've noticed that the bigger and sharper the food processor blade, the better it is for crushing graham crackers and cookies; making peanut butter from scratch; or chopping all the onions, carrots, and celery for a delicious-ass soup when you truly DGAF about chopping or cooking in bulk. (I totally can relate to that.) Take my advice: donate your mini food processor to the thrift store, and invest in one of the big ones. You'll thank me later. The big ones are definitely a little bulky, but it's worth making the room on your counter if you can.

Cast-iron skillet: I think the cast-iron skillet is very underrated. It's so versatile! It's not only useful for baking, frying, and grilling, but it also holds heat well and is easy to clean. The lifespan of cast-iron pans is longer than most other materials, and they're perfect for cook-to-serve recipes. My cast-iron is my go-to pan when I'm cooking at home, and I love to take it along when I go camping because the heat from the pan keeps food warm longer.

Kitchen scale: I used to be one of those people who cooked by eyeballing or "close enough-ing," especially when it came to measuring ingredients. I still am on certain occasions. But one thing (of many) my cooking experience has taught me is that a kitchen scale is an incredible aid, particularly when measuring ingredients by weight. The recipe writer took the time to measure their ingredients to the gram so you can have almost the exact results every time, environment permitting, so break out your scale.

Blender (and Grindr): You probably won't catch me on Grindr, but there's a very good chance you can find me blending or puréeing some bullshit. (Some blenders also have a food-processing function, so if you happen to have one of those, congrats on saving some counter space.) A high-powered blender can make just about anything creamier, which adds awesome texture to lots of dishes. I love using a blender for soups, smoothies, blended cocktails, ice cream, and more.

Vitamix owns the blender market, and for good reason: it's a really great blender. It can turn most things into a liquid or create a fluffy texture with little to no lumps in a matter of seconds. It also costs more than the first rolling pile of a vehicle that I bought in high school for the fearful price of $300. (It was a permanently dirty-looking little Volkswagen that couldn't physically move in reverse because the gear shift was missing. But that baby got me around town with no problem!) Something a tish more affordable might be the Ninja series. I like both!

A good grinder can go a long way if you like grinding your own coffee beans. I don't really drink coffee (I know...weird), but I can appreciate a good grinder that can grind other things like fresh peppercorns or any other spice blend I'm making.

Waffle iron: This is for the waffle people. (If you're a tried-and-true pancake person, you can skip to the next paragraph.) I like waffles because they're generally less messy to make than pancakes, and they're better for making a bomb-ass sandwich-type thing or a waffle log cabin à la *50 First Dates* with Drew Barrymore and Adam Sandler. Can't have a waffle without a waffle iron!

Pasta machine: Pasta machines are great if you love making fresh pasta. No doubt about that. That said, you absolutely can make fresh pasta with a rolling pin and a knife. The purpose of the machine is to help make things consistent for prettiest results. I would recommend asking for one as a gift, or disregard this altogether if you're not in your "homemade pasta-making era." Making pasta from scratch is obviously not as easy as cooking a box of dried pasta, but it can be fun, and the results are tasty.

Dutch oven: Dutch ovens are another multifunctional kitchen workhorse. I base some of my purchases on quality and how the item will look in my kitchen, but it also needs to get the job done. A little bit of research can go a long way with a really good-quality Dutch oven or braiser, but they can get pricey! Think of this tool like a cast-iron pan but in the form of a pot, with all the same uses but higher sides: use it to make soup, fry or boil chicken, bake bread—you get the point.

Baking dishes and sheets: It's true that I cannot fit a standard-size (full) baking sheet in my small apartment's oven, which is only slightly bigger than a vintage Easy-Bake Oven. But that doesn't mean you can't. Regardless of size, a rimmed baking sheet and a 9×13-inch (23×33cm) baking dish are baking essentials. A "rimmed" or "lipped" baking sheet (sometimes called a sheet pan) helps prevent messes while baking. A 9×13-inch (23×33cm) baking dish can hold a variety of dishes, from lasagna, to baked chicken or fish, to brownies.

Cutting boards and mats: I recommend a wooden cutting board for everything vegetable related and a plastic cutting board for all the proteins you can think of. Plastic is easier to clean, and when cutting raw meat and fish, cleanliness is very important. When it comes to baking, I recommend using a silicone mat instead of parchment paper, when possible, for quick cleanup and prevention of sticky messes.

Pots and pans: I have limited storage in my tiny kitchen, so I lean toward stackable, storable pots and pans, both nonstick and stainless steel. Pots that come with lids are always useful! When I was learning how to cook in my parents' kitchen, I was not allowed to use stainless steel until I mastered the nonstick and got the hang of what I was doing. I would recommend this practice so you're not sinking money into something you potentially could ruin if you're not familiar with it. Nonstick also saves you a lot of time scrubbing if you accidentally burn something.

Kitchen towels, potholders, and dishrags:
Towels, pot holders, and dishrags are must-haves...and they're probably the dirtiest items in your kitchen, so wash them often. I know a lot of people who like aesthetically pleasing dish towels—myself included—but here's a hack that will save you some serious coin: buy a bunch of paint towels from a local hardware store instead of higher-priced towels from a kitchen store. They absorb and clean up messes with no problem and they can be used for the rest of your household duties, too. I love them because they're relatively inexpensive and sold in bulk.

Mixing bowls: Various-sized mixing bowls are essential in every kitchen, and there are so many beautiful options to choose from. Scour garage sales and flea markets for classic vintage ones, or support a local potter whose work you love... with a teeny bit of research to ensure they're not lead based. (On a separate note: when you have a well-packed bowl, don't forget to share!)

Thermometers: Oven thermometers, instant-read thermometers, and frying/candy thermometers—they're all different, all useful, and all underrated. These temperature-takers make all the difference when you're baking, frying, or cooking things like jellies and jams.

One key kitchen tool that has never failed me—and that is too often overlooked and underused in the kitchen—is an oven thermometer. Having an accurate read on your oven temp can and will change your cooking game. Every oven is different, and many have hot spots. Varying temperatures can affect your results pretty drastically, so knowing your oven and its temperature can make or BAKE a dish. (See what I did there?) I always keep one in my oven so I can gauge things while I'm cooking.

Knives: The knives I use most often are a quality chef's knife, a paring knife, and a bread knife. It's your job to ensure that your knives are sharp, like your mind, and that you keep your fingers away from the blade. (Remember, knuckles up!)

Miscellaneous cooking and baking essentials for every kitchen:

- Cheese grater and microplane
- Rolling pin
- Wooden spoons
- Metal and rubber whisks and spatulas
- Pastry/pizza roller
- Strong and sturdy plastic or metal tongs
- Reusable chopsticks
- Colander
- Measuring cups and spoons
- Kitchen string
- Ruler (I like having a ruler close by to evenly measure dough when rolling it out to a specific thickness, so I can compare quickly for best results instead of eyeballing it.)

Cake decorating tools: If you're interested in cake decorating, I recommend getting piping bags, piping tips, offset spatulas of varying sizes, and a mini lazy Susan or a cake stand (or as my great grandma called them, a turntable). Sometimes decorating can feel like a chore, but it's more fun when you get the hang of it and learn a couple simple tips.

PANTRY PARTY

Here are the keys to my tiny kitchen kingdom! All the ingredients listed in this section are used in the recipes in this book. By no means am I telling you that you need to have all these items to be a successful cook, but they will give you a good start. And most if not all are easy to find. If I can buy these ingredients in my very small town, you should be able to source them where you live, too. I write recipes bearing in mind what should be accessible to everyone.

I get so jealous of warm places that have incredible produce year-round. Unfortunately, the cold is nothing to play with in North Dakota, so we turn to the next best affordable option. Can you guess what I'm going to say next? By using canned or frozen foods, you have access to ingredients that are out of season and can make delicious recipes all year long. Where I'm from, "good" greens can be incredibly challenging to find, considering it's cold six to eight months of the year. (A food desert can also look like a tundra.) Using canned or frozen greens solves the problem.

Growing up, I learned from my mom and my grandma that keeping a well-stocked pantry of dry canned and jarred goods is a great way to set yourself up for success. Having these items on hand means you can throw together some of your favorite dishes at the drop of a hat—and you'll always appear to be the host with the most because you don't have to run to the store for anything! If you do need something fresh, ask someone to pick it up on their way to you while they grab a bottle of wine or orange juice for brunch.

Pantry staples: In no specific order, some pantry basics that sort of speak for themselves are artichoke hearts, chickpeas (garbanzo beans), corn, allllll the beans (canned or dried), salsa, tomatoes, pickles (except bread and butter pickles, because, gross), olives (especially stuffed with bleu cheese or garlic), cocktail onions, anchovies, pie filling, puréed pumpkin, roasted red peppers, cocoa powder, cream of anything soup, and a variety of pickled vegetables.

Flour and grains: The variety of flours you keep on hand can change depending on what you do in your everyday life. Normally, I'll stick to good-quality all-purpose unbleached flour. (I like to use local flour when possible.) I also like to keep whole wheat flour, almond flour, and bread flour around. When making pizza dough, I recommend using 00 flour. It's not always available where I live, so all-purpose also gets the job done.

Spices, dried herbs, and other dry seasonings: It's easy to fill and forget your spice cabinet, but do yourself a favor and Marie Kondo it regularly. I usually will toss a spice if it's older than a year or so. When in doubt, use your sniffer: Does it still have a smell? Is the jar clean, or is it a little grimy looking? If it doesn't have a scent (or smells wrong) or if the jar is sketchy, toss it, replace it, and thank me later. I try to stick to the same brand of spices so they'll all fit in my very small cabinet. I also like to use glass jars because I can reuse them, adding new herbs I've dried myself or any leftover something or other, to take up less space.

Here's a list of spices, dried herbs, and other dry seasonings I usually have on hand: Italian seasoning (which you will see called for A LOT), herbs de Provence, parsley, dill, cilantro, chives, tarragon, cumin, lemon pepper, poultry seasoning, crushed red pepper flakes, onion powder, garlic powder, ground mustard, ground ginger, ground cinnamon, curry powder, black and white pepper, smoked paprika, allspice, whole nutmeg, Tajín, Old Bay Seasoning, buttermilk powder, ranch seasoning mix (for when I cannot be bothered to make my own; see page 212), French onion dip mix, and CHEESE POWDER. I'm sure I'm missing one or two others, but that's the gist of the list.

Bread: If I'm feeling lazy and going to buy bread instead of making it myself, I usually shoot for a crusty sourdough baguette (give it a light squeeze at the store to see if it's fresh), rye, or pumpernickel. You usually can tell the difference in quality between homemade and store-bought right off the bat, but who doesn't appreciate the convenience sometimes? Do what works best for your lifestyle.

Pasta: Certain pasta shapes are better for catching certain sauces. I recommend always keeping a variety of pasta and rice noodles (short and long) in your pantry. I'm not against having some cheese-filled frozen ravioli or tortellini within reach, either.

Rice: Rice is the best for wicking moisture out of a cell phone that took an accidental swim. It's also incredibly handy to have in your pantry. Its shelf life will blow away everything else in your cabinet. I like to keep jasmine, Arborio, and wild rice. Rice is great for rounding out pretty much every dish, and when in doubt, most things can be turned into a risotto.

Dairy and milk: In the recipes in this book that call for milk, I typically recommend full-fat cow's milk, but that doesn't mean you can't use what you have or prefer (especially if dairy isn't your thing). Sometimes nut milk yields an interesting flavor in a dish, for example. Just remember that fat is flavor. The same goes for sour cream, cream cheese, yogurt, and other dairy products.

Cheese: At any given point in time, you can find at least 12 to 16 types of cheese in my cheese drawer, and I hold that badge of honor proudly. My family and I are cheese heads, if being from Wisconsin didn't give it away already. Some cheeses to consider stocking include but are not limited to: Parmesan, Colby, Gruyère, mozzarella, burrata, cheddar, Swiss, Brie, cotija, queso fresco, and any Jack with a kick to it! The list could go on for pages. Cheese is probably the reason I would have a hard time going vegan. I'm low-key convinced "we," as in "the Midwest," all have dairy issues we just choose to ignore and instead "push through the pain." My lactose-intolerant peeps know what I mean. (Insert a disclaimer to see a medical professional and seek help.)

Butter: "Mo' butter is mo' better" is something that comes out of my mouth without me thinking about it. I prefer unsalted butter for cooking because I like to control the amount of salt I'm adding to a dish. You can use salted butter if you like; it's a personal preference, and a little more salt isn't the end of the world, so stick with what you know or what you regularly buy. You'll notice the difference in a good-quality butter. Kerrygold is a widely available premium brand that I prefer.

Hot stuff: Sorry, I should've been clearer: however hawt you may be, right now I'm referring to the spicy things I put on food. I keep a variety of hot sauces on hand because I love different peppers and levels of heat for different foods. You'll often find in my pantry sriracha, Tabasco, some sort of spicy truffle situation, crushed red pepper flakes, chili paste, or even just the classic Frank's RedHot hot sauce for something a little lower on the Scoville scale. One hot sauce I lean toward is Valentina. It's full of flavor, middle of the road heat-wise, great on everything, and most importantly, affordable! The perfect amount of heat can easily elevate a dish.

Herbs, greens, and produce: Cooking with fresh herbs is an easy way to improve the flavor of any recipe. (And one rule I love to follow as a food stylist is adding a pop of something green for garnish to a dish. Fresh herbs often fit that bill.) I grow fresh herbs in my kitchen year-round, and during the summer, I partner with my mom to plan and plant our garden. I always want tomatoes and basil and more dill than last year because of my unhealthy craving for dill. Between my kitchen and our garden, I aim to grow basil, parsley, thyme, rosemary, oregano, dill, and cilantro all year long. As for heartier greens, I usually recommend some sort of lettuce, arugula, spinach, mixed greens, kale, or cabbage. Alliums, the fancy word for the onion family (if you're a garlic girl, you probably already know that), shallots, scallions—I like to keep all of 'em on hand for just about everything. I have several different versions of garlic (fresh, frozen, pickled, pre-chopped) because I never want to run out!

Neutral oils: Vegetable and canola oil (i.e., flavorless oil) are widely available and inexpensive for use in baking or frying, plus they have a high smoke point, or the point at which an oil begins to smoke when it's heated. If you're not actively watching the temperature of your oil, it can be dangerous.

Olive oils: This is probably the ingredient I use the most often as I cook, and buying a better-quality olive oil DOES make a difference taste-wise. Don't spend outside your means (we're all trying to get that money, honey), but a somewhat good olive oil is essential. I learned about the difference when I worked on Molly's show. I like to use California olive oil because I believe it's the best quality available for its price point and is most widely available. Brightland is a delicious olive oil, and I especially like the flavors with a little heat added. Some people love avocado oil because of its smoke point and flavor in comparison to olive oil, which is valid. I'm an EVOO (extra-virgin olive oil) kinda guy, so Imma stick with that.

Vinegars: The acidic liquid that can ferment anything from apples to hooch! I love 'em. The vinegars I use the most often are balsamic vinegar or glaze, rice wine vinegar, apple cider vinegar, champagne vinegar, and distilled white vinegar.

Meats and proteins: I want you to use what's local and available to you. When making chicken (unless I'm preparing a whole chicken or wings), I tend to purchase breasts and thighs with the skin on. This is usually optional and won't affect the recipe too much if you prefer boneless skinless breasts and thighs (aside from not having all that delicious crunchy crispy skin). You can always break down a whole chicken if you'd like! I am a huge advocate of a good ol' cock (chicken—that's what the French call it; don't be a perv *wink*).

Ground beef, ground pork, chorizo, or dark meat ground turkey, are mostly interchangeable and follow the same cooking process, with some variation on the cook times. I prefer to buy sandwich meat over the counter at the deli while I dream about sandwich combinations. When purchasing bacon, I try to keep it unseasoned or somewhat smoked. This works just fine, but for good measure, try to avoid certain things if possible: no added sugar or nitrates or anything that is thin cut. I tend to stick to a medium to thick cut. If you don't like bacon, try prosciutto! It cooks a lot faster and doesn't have the same taste exactly but is similar enough and still delicious!

Eggs are another protein staple. I tend to use large eggs most often, but all my recipes are flexible when it comes to the types and sizes of eggs. When baking, I recommend bringing the eggs out of the fridge so they can come to room temperature or near it before using them in the recipe. I usually go through a dozen eggs in the span of a week, if not every other, but if you don't use them that quickly, eggs can last for a long time. To test if an egg is fresh, add it to a glass of water. If it sinks, it's fresh. If it floats, it's developed too much air inside the shell and might be spoiled.

Fish and seafood: I enjoy fresh seafood from time to time when I make a trip to Wisconsin or go on a fishing trip with friends, but frozen from the grocery store works just fine too. When buying from the store, I'll shoot for wild-caught peeled and cleaned skrimp (shrimp), salmon, mussels, and lobster. Sales at the market usually happen when foods are in season; if the store has plenty of something, chances are it will go on sale, so it's good to keep that in mind.

Protein and dairy alternatives: Plant-based "meats" have come a long way in recent years, and even if you aren't vegetarian or vegan, you can still eat—and might actually like!—some of these alternatives. (Dad, I'm calling you out here.) Some of these plant-based foods can be a great replacement for when you don't feel like running to the store ...or you're snowed in, like I usually am! And not to be that guy, but these foods also help the planet a little bit by creating a smaller carbon footprint. I've purposely designed the recipes in this book with the flexibility to substitute plant-based proteins as you like. Substituting can change the taste slightly, but the dish will still be great! Plant-based proteins such as Beyond Meat, tofu, mushrooms, seitan, nuts, beans, and potatoes are some great alternatives to try.

I mentioned nut milks earlier, but that's not the only dairy alternative you can use. For example, coconut cream works as a great substitute for heavy whipping cream in most scenarios. I especially love using it when making a sheet pan soup. Some dairy-free cheeses are available. I like to think of nutritional yeast as the Parmesan of the vegan world. As for eggs, a "flax egg," which is a combination of flaxseed meal and water, can be used in place of a chicken's egg when vegan baking. It probably won't have the same rise you'd get from an chicken egg, but it'll still taste lovely.

JUST THE TIP(S)

All of the tips, tricks, and hacks that will set you up for success on your culinary trek to Mordor.

Read the recipe: This might be my most helpful tip. Before you even start to think about cooking a recipe, read it all the way through once. Then read it again. Did you read it? Good, now read it once more for good measure. I know this sounds like a "duh" thing, but it will dramatically change the way you cook. This method always yields the best results (speaking for a friend who has messed up a lot of recipes).

Mise en place (a.k.a. get your shit together): Gather all the ingredients, and put them in one place, measured and prepared according to what the recipe requires or to the best of your ability. I call this act "pulling trays" because that's what I learned to do while working on set for the Food Network—I got a sheet tray and filled it with all the ingredients and tools required for a recipe. Then all you have to do when you're ready to start cooking is follow along with the recipe. Ta-da!

Keep an organized, running grocery list: In addition to keeping a well-stocked pantry, I suggest you keep an organized and running grocery list. I also do this when I am planning for meals to be sure I have everything I need without having to run to the store for a missing ingredient.

Life hack tomato sauce: When you're tight on cash, like I was when I was in college and most of my twenties, or if you're out of your favorite jarred sauce, I recommend grabbing a can of whole tomatoes (which are much cheaper than jarred sauce), puréeing them in a blender, and then adding crushed garlic, minced onion, and fresh or dried herbs, salt, and whatever other flavors you fancy. Stir and simmer over low heat until you're ready to use the sauce. This is a great hack from my mom, who could always work magic on canned tomatoes.

Use an oven thermometer: (No, this is not the same as a meat thermometer, but sometimes they can be both if you've got some groovy equipment.) One essential kitchen tool that has never failed me—and that is too often overlooked and underused in the kitchen—is an oven thermometer. Every oven is different, and many have hot spots. Varying temperatures can affect your results pretty drastically, so knowing your oven and its temperature can make or BAKE a dish. (See what I did there?) I always keep one in my oven, so I can gauge things while I'm cooking.

Sharpen your knives: Would you like a set of fancy new stitches at the ER? Then keep using a dull knife—I do NOT dare you! Sorry, but it really does bear repeating: be safe and protect your digits as well as your purchase (the knives), by taking care of them. Be sharp, like your knives. They're a tool and one of your besties in the kitchen, but they're also a weapon.

Just add salt: Salt is very important for flavor. I stick to using coarse kosher salt and don't really stray far from it. I believe it melts evenly into dishes while still adding a few more minerals than we normally consume (and low-key kind of need). When I call for salt in these recipes, I'm calling for coarse kosher salt unless otherwise specified. I use Diamond Crystal. (Morton works just fine, but it's just a touch saltier to me.) Maldon sea salt flakes, also called finishing salt, is what I use when I want to be a little fancy while finishing a dish!

A pinch of salt is different for everyone—and can be dramatically different it seems. I measure a pinch of salt by pinching with my thumb, index, and middle fingers. The most important thing is to taste as you go, seasoning at different parts of the dish, so you don't overdo it.

Reduce, reuse, recycle, Rihanna! (Best said by Ilana Glazer of *Broad City*.): Save all the scraps from every onion you chop, all the garlic bits, the pepper parts, the tomato seeds, the celery stalks, and the carrot tops until you have enough to make a delicious homemade vegetable stock. If you learn to break down a chicken, you'll save tons by making your own chicken broth from the cuttings. After you've mastered those tasks, maybe someday I'll teach you how to can, jar, and preserve things, you little wannabe homesteader, you!

Try a quick pickle: I never throw out the brine from pickles. One way to make pickled onions with little effort is by thinly slicing an onion (or two, depending on how much brine you've got) and adding it to the jar after I've finished the pickles, let it sit overnight, and you're in business! Or try adding some brine to some of your sauces that need a little vinegar or acidity. I promise you'll love it.

Grow your own (aka we've got food at home): Did you know that you can continue to regrow some produce you get from the grocery store or farmers market? For example, you can grow green onions, avocados, lemons (if you've got years and the patience to grow one), garlic, celery, and even fresh herbs if there are a few roots showing. For most of these items, you can just pop the seeds or pit in some water, place it near a sunny window, and it will do the work itself until you're ready to use it or plant it in soil. And in the words of Lil Wayne (mostly), "Save you some moolah baybee!"

Embrace the "garbage bowl": Use a "garbage bowl" when you're chopping and getting all fancy in the kitchen. Have ONE bowl for all the scraps of things you can't repurpose or simply won't use—eggshells, produce trimmings, among other bits and things. Hear me out: instead of 87 million trips to the trash can, throw it all in the garbage bowl and then toss it out once. (Not the bowl itself, just everything inside it.) I prefer to call it a "thanks for coming bowl" like Anne Burrell to make it sound less as if I pulled the bowl from the garbage.

This is also great motivation to clean as you go, which can be a time-saver. I know it's annoying and dumb, and I don't want to do it either. So here's my proposition: while something is cooking for 5 to 10 minutes, you can do the dishes...or make the other person who plans on eating the meal do the dishes. Now that's what I call balance!

Wash while you work: Throughout the writing of this book, I did not have a dishwasher. (My tiny old kitchen didn't have the hookups for it, I was renting and couldn't add the hookups, and besides, I was broke.) Therefore, I hand-washed all the dishes used for testing—more than 1,000 dishes—and no, this is not an exaggeration. I don't like to use the word hate often, but I HATE doing dishes. Why am I complaining about this here? I just needed to vent now that I have an audience. (Insert maniacal laughter.) You'll be pleased to know that I now have a dishwasher. (Everyone start to slow clap. I'll wait.) If you have time, do the dishes during passive cooking time, or while waiting for things to cool off. I don't know the science behind it, but Scrub Daddy is possibly the best sponge out there in my opinion, (non spons). It's so handy to have a sponge change texture from coarse to soft just based on the temperature of the water. If you're stuck washing dishes the old-fashioned way, I recommend grabbing your laptop and catching on your favorite reality television shows or pop on an audiobook or podcast to pass the time.

Putting out a grease fire: I'm like a gay Smokey Bear, helping everyone prevent kitchen fires. First, never add water to hot oil. That is the quickest way to start a grease fire. If you have a grease fire, cover the pot with a METAL lid. If you don't have a lid, use a baking sheet or something similar that will completely cover the pan and the flames—no oxygen = no fire—then safely remove the pot from the heat. Make sure to NEVER put out a grease fire with water. Baking soda can smother the flames if you can't get a lid or baking sheet. Obviously, you should call the fire department if needed. And of course make sure to have a viable fire extinguisher in the house (they can expire, so pay attention).

1

BREKKIE, DRAG BRUNCH & LUNCH

TRADITION

Tradition for my family is about simply being together. While growing up in the Haas house—or as I like to call it, the "Haas Haus"—my parents enforced the rule that everyone would eat dinner together. We would wait until everyone was home to sit down and eat, which really meant a lot to me. Granted, we couldn't always do this, but it felt so wonderful to take that time together to share about our days before we all went back to the busy bustle that was our household.

When I was younger, my family decided that what worked best for us as a family unit during Christmastime was to take a less traditional approach to the usual festivities. My parents were always busy working in retail during those months, and one very small sacrifice I contributed was to stay home and babysit my siblings after school and on the weekends. Naturally, I didn't appreciate this at the time, but looking back, I can say I truly enjoyed it. My parents would still somehow pull out all the stops, decorating, buying gifts, and planning meals. As a family, we decided we were a little fed up with "the norm" and just wanted to spend time together. So we passed on the big, fancy dinner with all the fixin's to make the most of our time with each other.

The first year we decided to celebrate with a trip to Blockbuster (RIP), which led to an entire day of doing puzzles, playing board games, and watching movies together in comfortable pajamas. For food, we had a spread of appetizers and bites along the lines of little smokies, fried pickles, nachos, a charcuterie board, and of course, some vegetables. I HIGHLY recommend you try it. Or make your own theme! We've since moved on to themed holiday dinners, such as crawdad Cajun boils for New Year's Eve and Italian Christmas, build-your-own-pizza bars for birthdays, seafood Easters (with everything down to cheddar bay biscuits), and even slurping soup for the big "souper bowl" game. I cannot wait to become a dad so I can share some of those holiday traditions with my future children.

Some people don't like to stray from the traditions that were passed down from previous generations, and that's totally fine. I like to think of life as a literal melting pot for food and people. (But just to be clear: not in a cannibalistic way.) Just try to remember that you can create your own version of "traditional."

Throughout this book, you'll find a combination of "modern" recipes and some of my favorite classic dishes, all with a personal touch, bringing new meaning to some of my favorite traditions.

BREAKFAST & BRUNCH

Frosted Cinnamon Caramel Rolls

SERVES 4-6 (IF PEOPLE HAVE 2), MAKES ABOUT 9 ROLLS
PREP TIME: 10 MINUTES
TOTAL TIME: 2 HOURS 30 MINUTES (PLUS 1 HOUR 30 MINUTES RISING TIME)

I solemnly swear that these are my all-time favorite cinnamon rolls. In fact, I have a funny story about the first time I made them. Imagine me just doodle-bopping in my little kitchen on a sunny afternoon. I was with one of my best friends, Mary, who was doing homework at my apartment while I was testing this recipe. Mary had volunteered to be my taste tester for the day, and I joined her at the table, ready to "evaluate" the rolls—scientifically, of course.

Less than a minute into peeling back the warm, soft layers of bread with their pillowy frosting-lined tops, a whole giant roll had vanished down my gullet. I had inhaled it. I still laugh every time I remember the look of shock on Mary's face, as she was in the middle of telling a story while witnessing the event, and asking, "Are you okay??? I've never seen someone eat so quickly...anddd those are giant!" My response? Uncontrollable belly laughter! I just couldn't help it. These are so lovely! But please don't be like me. Savor and enjoy every crumb of these sure-to-be brunch staples.

For the dough

3½–4 cups all-purpose flour, plus extra for dusting

½ teaspoon ground cardamom

Freshly grated nutmeg (3–4 passes) or a few shakes of ground nutmeg

1× ¾-ounce (21g) packet of active dry yeast

½ tablespoon granulated sugar

2 eggs

1 cup warm water or milk

1 tablespoon vegetable or olive oil

For the filling

1× stick unsalted butter, divided in half and softened

¼ cup granulated sugar

½ cup light or dark brown sugar

1 teaspoon ground cinnamon

1 teaspoon ground cardamom

For the frosting

1× 8-ounce (226g) block of cream cheese

2 cups powdered sugar (or less if you like a glaze)

Pinch of salt

¼ teaspoon ground cinnamon

¼ teaspoon cardamom

¼ teaspoon ground ginger

1 teaspoon vanilla extract

Teeny tiny drop of almond extract (optional)

Drizzle of heavy cream (if you like a thinner frosting)

About ¼ cup store-bought caramel for topping (or however much you like)

Special equipment

Stand mixer with the dough hook

Rolling pin

1. Add all the dough ingredients to the bowl of a stand mixer fitted with the dough attachment. Mix for 6 to 10 minutes or until the dough appears sticky and pulls away from the edges of the bowl. If you don't have a stand mixer or a dough attachment, add all the ingredients to a large bowl and whisk for 6 to 10 minutes. Switch to a rubber spatula to mix for 6 to 8 minutes. Turn out the dough onto your counter, and knead for about 10 minutes or until you have a smooth dough.

2. Transfer the dough to a large, oiled bowl, cover and let it rise in a warm place for 1 hour or until doubled in size.

3. Turn out dough onto a floured surface, and evenly roll with a rolling pin until it's the size of a 9×13-inch (23×33cm) baking sheet.

4. For the filling, use a spatula to spread the softened butter evenly over the dough and then evenly sprinkle the granulated sugar, brown sugar, cinnamon, and cardamom over the entire surface, all the way to the edges. With the long side of the dough facing you, roll it over and onto itself until a tightly packed log is formed. It should be about 12 inches (30.5cm) long.

5. Using a serrated knife, cut the log into 1- or 2-inch (2.5–5cm) pieces, depending on how many you'd like to make. Start by cutting it through the middle, so you have two equal logs. Then cut each smaller log into as many rolls as you would like to serve. Remember, they will double in size as they rise and bake, so cut a bit smaller than the size you want the finished rolls to be.

6. Assemble the cut rolls in the dish with the prettier side facing up. Cover with a clean cloth, and let rise in a warm place for 30 minutes to 1 hour. You'll know when they're ready because they will have doubled in size and touch the edges of the pan.

7. While the rolls are rising, preheat the oven to 350°F (180°C). Spray a 9×13-inch (23×33cm) casserole dish with cooking spray.

8. Bake for 25 to 30 minutes.

9. Meanwhile, using a stand mixer with the paddle attachment, whip together all the frosting ingredients except the caramel for no more than 5 minutes. If you don't have a stand mixer, add all the frosting ingredients except the caramel to a large bowl. Using a whisk, whip the frosting for 8 to 10 minutes.

10. Remove the rolls from the oven and allow to cool in the pan for 10 minutes and then generously frost. Drizzle with caramel, and serve immediately. Enjoy!

······················· TIP ·······················

The dough can be made overnight and left to rise in the fridge or covered on the kitchen counter in a warm place.

Gas Station Breakfast Pizza

SERVES 4-6 | PREP TIME: 10 MINUTES | TOTAL TIME: 35 MINUTES

During the winters in Grand Forks, when it's extra cold—say, about –30°F (–1°C) with a wind chill of –60°F (–51°C) or some outrageous number—it goes without saying that you need something hot to eat. So... have you ever gotten a gas station breakfast pizza on your morning commute gas fill-up? It's what I crave on those mornings because it's salty and meaty and filling and gives me the firepower to get the day started. I'm quite literally obsessed with it.

This version is easy to make at home, is always a real hit at brunch (speaking from experience), and is great for a hangover (also speaking from experience)! The only part you need to plan for is waiting for the dough to rise, but you can use your favorite store-bought dough if the spirit moves you! This recipe has breakfast sausage and gravy as the sauce, but feel free to substitute with other toppings if you prefer. This also totally works great with plant-based sausage. I hope this fuels your body and that you have a day just as wonderful as you are!

Cooking spray, for greasing (optional)

All-purpose flour, for dusting

½ pound (225g) bacon (about 4–6 slices), or more for snacking (see page 48)

1 pound (450g) Homemade Pizza Dough (see page 210) or store-bought pizza dough

4 tablespoons unsalted butter

3 large eggs

1 pound (450g) hot Italian sausage

1 tablespoon Italian seasoning

1 teaspoon crushed red pepper flakes (optional)

1 teaspoon fresh or dried sage

1 tablespoon light brown sugar

3 tablespoons all-purpose flour

4 garlic cloves, minced

1 cup whole milk

1 cup shredded cheese of choice (I like to use a cheddar blend), divided

2–3 green onions, thinly sliced

Special equipment

Rolling pin

1. Preheat the oven to 350°F (180°C). Lightly coat a baking sheet (if using) with cooking spray. Or make sure you have enough flour on the bottom of your pizza to easily remove from the pan.

2. Arrange the bacon in a single layer on a separate rimmed baking sheet fitted with a baking rack, and bake for 15 to 20 minutes. When the bacon is done to your desired crispiness, transfer it to a paper towel–lined plate. Crumble or cut the bacon into small pieces, and set aside.

3. Lightly flour your work surface, and use a rolling pin to roll out the Homemade Pizza Dough to fit the baking sheet you're using. Gently transfer the dough to the prepared baking sheet.

4. In a large saucepan over medium heat, add about a tablespoon of the butter along with the eggs, and cook, whipping up a little scramble, for 3 to 5 minutes or until the eggs are just set. Transfer the scrambled eggs to a clean plate. (It's okay if they are a little wet. They are going to bake in the oven later.)

5. To make the gravy-type sauce, in a large saucepan over medium heat, add the sausage, Italian seasoning, crushed red pepper flakes, if using, sage, cloves, and brown sugar. Mix well, and brown the meat for 5 to 8 minutes. Transfer the meat to a plate, and set aside.

6. To the pan, add the rest of the butter and allow to melt. Add the all-purpose flour and garlic, and stir until a thick paste is formed. Pour in the milk and half of the cheese, and mix until smooth. Pour over the pizza dough and spread to an even layer.

7. Top the sauce with the remaining cheese, followed by the sausage, bacon, and scrambled eggs.

8. Bake for 25 minutes or until the crust has started to turn golden, the cheese is melty and bubbly, and the eggs are done to your desired firmness.

9. Remove from the oven and let cool for a few minutes on the baking sheet. Top with green onions and serve. Enjoy!

For the mimosas

1× 24-ounce (750ml) bottle champagne of choice, or nonalcoholic sparkling wine, chilled (I like it sweet)

½ ounce (15ml) orange juice or your choice juice, or to taste

½–1 ounce (15–30ml) vodka (you can use flavored vodka if you want)

For the fruit dip

1× 8-ounce (225g) block cream cheese, softened

1× 7.5-ounce (213g) jar marshmallow fluff

3 tablespoons maraschino cherries, with some juice

Chopped fruits (honeydew, cherries, cantaloupe, strawberries, watermelon, pineapple, oranges or whatever your heart desires!)

Special equipment

Funnel or pitcher

Mimosas...with Fruit Dip!

SERVES 2-4 AND THE FRUIT WILL SERVE MORE!
PREP TIME: 5 MINUTES (OR 10 IF YOU'RE CUTTING A BUNCH OF FRUIT)
TOTAL TIME: 5 MINUTES (OR 10 IF YOU'RE CUTTING A BUNCH OF FRUIT)

Is it even a drag brunch if there's not an all-you-can-drink mimosa on the menu? Maybe! But it probably won't be as much fun (not to imply you'll only have fun if you're drinking). Of course, this isn't quite a meal, but it is the main course at many brunches. I find that when drinking adult beverages, it's good to get a little something in your stomach before the festivities begin (speaking from countless painful hangover experiences), so this drink comes with a snack. And be sure to hydrate, y'all! If you simply cannot be bothered to cut the fruit for this recipe, you can buy it precut. Please drink responsibly!

1. **Pitcher method:** Into a pitcher, pour the champagne, orange juice, and vodka, and give it a light mix. **Bottle method:** Pour a small amount of the champagne out into a glass to make room for the other ingredients. Using a funnel, pour the orange juice and vodka into the bottle and give it a light swirl.

2. For the dip, in a small bowl, mix together the cream cheese, marshmallow fluff, and maraschino cherries, with a little bit of the cherry juice, using a whisk or electric mixer. Serve immediately with the remaining fruit arranged around the dip. Enjoy!

> **TIPS**
>
> You can add some ice to the pitcher if you're drinking outside, but it will water down the mimosas.
>
> You also can add some little garnishes to the pitcher. For example, are you using orange juice? If so, float some orange slices in the pitcher.
>
> For those trying to get extra turnt, you can increase the amount of vodka. This will help make it feel like you're really at a drag show where the drinks are more burnt!
>
> If you're not serving right away, keep the dip and fruit cold until ready to serve.

Tomato Skillet with Pesto

SERVES 6-8 | PREP TIME: 5 MINUTES | TOTAL TIME: 30 MINUTES

This dish has so many names in so many cultures: eggs in purgatory, shakshuka, and menemen, to name a few. And if it isn't already apparent that I'm obsessed with tomato and basil flavors, I decided to put my own twist on this dish by pairing it with one of my favorite things: PESTO! This is one of my internet favorite dishes, and I call it my "breakfast after you've had a perfect date." Or the dish to make for your friends to spill the tea while eating an amazing brunch. One of my best friends, Anna, is known for hating tomatoes. After trying this, she fell in love and now makes it every other week or whenever I come to visit!

This is also one of my STAPLE brunch recipes because it takes so little effort. You probably have everything you need on hand already, it's ready in no time, it feeds a small crowd, but most importantly, it's extraordinarily great for dipping into with any carby vessel and then applying to your face.

2 tablespoons extra-virgin olive oil

1 large white or yellow onion, roughly chopped

6–8 garlic cloves, minced

4 tablespoons tomato paste

1–2 teaspoons crushed red pepper flakes, or to taste, plus extra for garnish (optional)

½ tablespoon Italian seasoning

1 teaspoon ground ginger

½ teaspoon ground mustard

1 teaspoon ground cumin

1 tablespoon sweet paprika

Salt and freshly ground black pepper

2× 26-ounce (740g) cans chopped tomatoes

6–8 large eggs

4–6 tablespoons Delishaas Pesto (see page 127) or store-bought pesto

Drizzle extra-virgin olive oil

Handful of feta, ½ bunch roughly chopped fresh cilantro or parsley, for garnish

1–2 baguettes, sliced and lightly toasted, for serving

1. In a large pot or braiser set over medium heat, add the olive oil, onion, and garlic, and cook for about 5 to 10 minutes or until soft and translucent.

2. Add the tomato paste, crushed red pepper flakes, Italian seasoning, ginger, ground mustard, cumin, and paprika. Cook for about 5 minutes, add the chopped tomatoes, salt, and pepper, then bring to a simmer.

3. When the sauce is starting to simmer slightly, crack the eggs on top, one at a time, spacing them about 1 inch (2.5cm) apart.

4. Cover and cook for 5 to 7 minutes for perfectly jammy eggs, or longer if you like your yolks firm.

5. Top with the pesto and extra-virgin olive oil. Garnish with the feta, cilantro or parsley, and more crushed red pepper flakes, if using. Serve with hunks of toasted bread or your choice of carby vessel, and apply to face. Enjoy!

For the batter

2 cups all-purpose flour

2 tablespoons granulated sugar

2 teaspoons baking powder

2 cups whole milk

3 tablespoons unsalted butter, melted, plus extra for serving

2 eggs

1 teaspoon vanilla extract

Dash of ground cinnamon (optional)

For the filling

12 ounces (340g) ricotta (any fat percentage)

½ cup fresh blueberries, plus extra for garnish

1 teaspoon poppy seeds

1 tablespoon fresh thyme leaves

1 lemon, zested and juiced, zest reserved for garnish

3 tablespoons honey, plus extra for garnish

Whipped cream, for garnish

Special equipment

Waffle iron

Blueberry-Stuffed Belgian Waffles

SERVES 6-8 | PREP TIME: 5 MINUTES | TOTAL TIME: 30 MINUTES

This might sound incredibly specific, but do you remember staying at a hotel as a kid, after swimming in the pool all evening, and waking up to the joy of a hopefully good-quality continental breakfast waffles? This recipe is a level up from a hotel waffle—which sounds silly, I know—with my spin on a jammy, sweet-but-creamy filling. It'll make you feel the best kind of bougie! You can prepare this dish in your robe while pretending you're at a five-star hotel. Enjoy!

1. In a large bowl, mix together all the batter ingredients. Set aside to rest for 10 minutes while you prepare everything else.

2. Preheat the waffle iron.

3. In a separate large bowl, combine the ricotta, blueberries, poppy seeds, thyme, lemon juice, and honey.

4. When the waffle iron is hot, lightly coat it with cooking spray.

5. Pour about ¼ to ½ cup batter onto the iron (depending on how big your waffle iron is; I recommend starting with ¼ cup), top with a healthy scoop of the filling (about ¼ cup), followed by another scoop of batter (another ¼ cup). Close the waffle iron, and cook for about 5 to 10 minutes. Lift the lid a bit if needed to check on the waffle when you can smell it toasting.

6. When it's ready, the waffle will come off the iron easily. If it still wants to stay in its little cast-iron bed, let it continue to cook for a few more minutes. It should be golden with maybe a few little brown spots of crispiness around the edges. Transfer the cooked waffle to a plate, and repeat with the remaining batter and filling.

7. Garnish the waffles with your desired toppings and a little bit more filling if you'd like, along with a pat of butter, whipped cream, honey or syrup, and lemon zest, and serve immediately. Enjoy!

> **TIP**
>
> You can totally cheat this recipe by using your favorite pancake or waffle mix. Trader Joe's is probably my favorite mix, but this also works with protein pancakes, my fellow gym rats!

Mammoth Muffins

MAKES 6 MAMMOTH-SIZED MUFFINS OR 12 REGULAR-SIZED MUFFINS
PREP TIME: 10 MINUTES | TOTAL TIME: 35 MINUTES

Muffins are probably the dark horse (not the Katy Perry kind) of bakeries and grocery stores. Just so we're all on the same page, muffins are really just cakes, and pancakes are also just cakes, thus the name, right? (Not to get into the same line of thinking as, "Is a hot dog a sandwich, or is everything is a sandwich?") Anyway, when I was in high school, I used to be a bag boy at the local grocery store. Just about every break, I would get a fresh muffin from the bakery. It was a problem I'm clearly not over, BUT these are better than a grocery store muffin and I MEAN IT! I'm going to show you how to make them with a delightful streusel topping, because everyone knows the most delicious part of a muffin is the top. This was one of the first treats I made for everyone when I worked on Molly Yeh's show, and it was a big hit! It's also super easy to make vegan for those who are so inclined.

For the batter

Cooking spray or butter, for greasing

1 large egg

½ cup whole milk (this is also great with buttermilk)

½ cup vegetable or olive oil

2 teaspoons vanilla extract

2 cups all-purpose flour

¼ cup granulated sugar

¼ cup brown sugar, lightly packed

2 teaspoons baking powder

Pinch of salt

Dash of ground cinnamon or cardamom (optional)

2× 6-ounce (170g) chocolate bars of choice, roughly chopped (I like Tony's Chocolonely with caramel bits), or 1½ cups fruit of choice

For the topping

½ cup granulated sugar

¼ cup all-purpose flour

1 teaspoon almond extract (optional)

4–6 tablespoons unsalted butter, cold

Special equipment

Muffin pan

Cupcake liners

1. Preheat the oven to 400°F (200°C). Line a cupcake or muffin pan with liners, and lightly coat any remaining parts of the pan that are exposed with cooking spray (or grease with butter before adding the liners).

2. In a large bowl, whisk together the egg, milk, vegetable oil, and vanilla extract.

3. In a separate bowl, lightly whisk together the all-purpose flour, granulated sugar, brown sugar, baking powder, salt, and cinnamon, if using. Don't skip whisking; it's important to distribute the baking powder!

4. Slowly add the dry ingredients to the wet, and whisk until the mixture is slightly lumpy, kind of like a very loose cookie dough. Add the chocolate, and mix until combined.

5. In the bowl used for the dry ingredients, add the topping ingredients. Using your hands or a fork, combine the ingredients and crumble together the sugar and flour with the butter. When it's done, it will look like a clumpy bowl of sawdust with little pea-sized balls, which is the butter coated in sugar and flour.

6. Evenly divide the batter among the muffin tins, filling them just to the rim, not halfway like most recipes. Add a hefty spoonful of the topping on top. (Be sure it all stays in the liner. It will spill out on its own as the muffins bake.) Use all the topping, spreading it evenly among all the muffins.

7. Bake for 25 minutes, checking for doneness at 20 minutes. You will know right away by the size if they're ready to come out because the muffins will be overflowing (in a good way). The tops should be golden, and if they separate a little, that's totally okay. They'll still taste awesome. Let the muffins cool in the pan until ready to serve. Enjoy!

.... **TIPS** ....

I know we're using liners, but we're also going to spray the pan because these muffins are purposely going to overflow, and we don't want the muffin top to stick to the sides. So be sure to cover all the surfaces around the tins with spray or butter. Just trust the process!

If you want regular-sized muffins—boring, but still okay—only fill the muffin tins half full. Or, if you want even larger muffins, you can let the batter sit for 10 to 15 minutes before baking, which will increase the size slightly larger than usual.

You can substitute the chocolate for 1 cup of fresh fruit, such as blueberries. To make the batter vegan, use vegan butter, dairy-free milk, a flax egg, and vegan chocolate.

Full English-American Breakfast

SERVES 6-8
PREP TIME: 5 MINUTES | TOTAL TIME: 45 MINUTES

Breakfast is the most important meal of the day. I don't know if that's scientifically true or not, but it makes me feel like I have less to worry about if I've started my day with a meal that will keep me full until dinner. This is the combination of foods that always feel like home to me, which includes both English and American brekkie staples.

This is a crowd pleaser because it's a crowd feeder, and did I mention you can do it all in two pans? I simply love making a breakfast feast like this because this method is probably the easiest way to make breakfast for any size group of people with a TON of options.

1 pound (450g) thick bacon (the thickest you can find)

12 ounces (340g) breakfast sausage links or patties

6 large eggs

4 tablespoons unsalted butter

20 ounces (560g) fresh or frozen hash browns

Salt and freshly ground black pepper

Olive oil (optional)

6-7 ounces (150-180g) baby bella or button mushrooms, stem removed or trimmed

10-11 ounces (283-300g) vine-ripened tomatoes

1× 15-ounce (425g) can baked beans (Heinz brand in tomato sauce if you can find it)

Grated Parmesan and chopped fresh parsley, for garnish

Serve with

Toasted bread of choice (I recommend sourdough), sliced avocado, ketchup, and hot sauce

1. In a large skillet over medium-high heat, and working in batches, fry the bacon and sausage for about 10 minutes or until browned and cooked through. (Or toss the bacon in the oven using the handy trick I mentioned on page 48 to save some stovetop space). Transfer to a paper towel–lined plate, cover, and set aside. Save the grease from the meats in the skillet.

2. Add the eggs to the skillet, and fry for about 5 minutes or to your preferred doneness. Transfer the eggs to a clean plate. (If needed, you can put anything you want to keep warm in the microwave or on a baking sheet in the oven.)

3. In a second large skillet over low to medium heat, add 2 tablespoons butter along with the hash browns in an even layer and season with salt and pepper. This should be kind of like a potato pancake; you can cut it into four sections and flip over each when it's developed a dark brown color. You're shooting for crispy edges, so check after about 5 minutes and flip after 10 minutes, adding more butter if needed. Cook for 5 to 10 minutes on the other side. Transfer to a plate.

4. Toast your bread, either in the pan you used for the eggs or in a toaster. (Put your youngest diner to work learning how to toast!) If using the pan method, melt the remaining 2 tablespoons of butter in the pan and then add the bread and toast for 2 to 4 minutes per side. If using a toaster, spread with the remaining 2 tablespoons butter after toasting.

5. A vegetable-inspired series is needed for all this delicious protein. Dry the pan, and set it over medium heat. Add the olive oil, if using, followed by the mushrooms and tomatoes, and season with salt and pepper. Cook for 5 to 10 minutes. You just want the tomatoes to blister and start to release some of their juices. This can be served in the pan.

6. Add the baked beans to the skillet, set over medium heat, and cook for 6 to 8 minutes or until warm. You can serve the beans in the skillet, too. Garnish the beans with freshly grated Parmesan and parsley, and serve everything with a side of toast. Enjoy!

> **TIP**
>
> For little kids who want to help prepare this feast, I recommend starting them off toasting and buttering the bread. It sounds silly, but it's extremely helpful and then you don't have to multitask as much.

Dutch Baby Pancakes

SERVES 4-6 | PREP TIME: 5 MINUTES | TOTAL TIME: 30 MINUTES

Dutch baby pancakes are a reminder of a warm and welcoming part of my childhood. I was introduced to them probably before I was forming improper compound sentences. There's nothing better than waking up on a Sunday morning with rays of golden, glowing sun shining on your sheets and an open window pumping in crisp, fresh air and birdsong. While making your way down to the kitchen, all you have to do is follow the hallways faintly perfumed from the baking skillet cakes... and the sound of the whirring blender. Ahhh, to be face to face with fresh, hot, and buttery Dutch baby pancakes, ready to eat directly from the skillet, with a world of endless possibilities for toppings. My favorites are warm cooked apples and loads of cinnamon, sugar, or syrup and whipped cream. It's like a fluffy bunny in the form of a puffy pancake, but with crispy edges and your favorite toppings...what more could you ask for?

1. Preheat the oven to 450°F (230°C).

2. In your skillet or oven-safe pan, add 2 to 3 tablespoons of butter. Pop the skillet in the oven while you prep everything else.

3. In a blender, add the eggs, milk, vanilla extract, 3 tablespoons of butter, flour, salt, granulated sugar, if using, and nutmeg. Cover, and blend for 3 to 4 minutes. If you don't have a blender, you can add the wet ingredients to a large bowl, followed by the dry ingredients, and whisk for 5 to 6 minutes or until very well combined.

4. By this time, the butter should be melted in the skillet. Remove the skillet from the oven. Carefully swirl the butter around the pan and the edges, and pour in the batter. Place the skillet back in the oven, and bake for about 20 minutes. Check on it at the 15-minute mark.

5. Meanwhile, in a medium pan over low to medium heat, add 2 more tablespoons of butter along with the apples, cinnamon, and brown sugar. Cook, stirring, for 5 to 10 minutes and then remove from the heat. The topping mixture will be very hot, so don't go dipping in any piggies.

6. When the pancake is done, it might be a little strange looking—puffy and golden brown with crispy edges—but that's okay! Remove the skillet from the oven. Don't worry when the pancake shrinks a bit. Give it a little rub with some of the remaining butter along with a healthy scoop of the apple topping. Sprinkle with confectioners' sugar, dollop on whipped cream, and/or drizzle with your favorite syrup, if using, and serve. Enjoy!

For the batter

¾ cup unsalted butter, softened, divided

4 eggs

1 cup milk of choice, at room temperature

2 teaspoons vanilla extract

1¾ cups all-purpose flour

Pinch of salt

3 tablespoons granulated sugar (optional)

Freshly grated nutmeg (3–4 passes) or a few shakes of ground nutmeg

For the topping

3–4 apples, diced or cut into thin slices (any kind of apple works great, but I lean toward Honeycrisps for this)

Dash of ground cinnamon

Serve with

⅓ cup light brown sugar, lightly packed

Sifted confectioners' sugar, whipped cream, and/or syrup, for serving (optional)

Special equipment:

9- or 12-inch (23 or 30 cm) skillet or oven-safe pan

Blender

.... **TIPS** ....

You can use your favorite apples for the topping. Or in place of the apple topping, you can use fresh fruit.

The key to this recipe lies in buttering the pan very well so the pancake can climb up the edges to brown.

Drizzle of olive oil

1 white or yellow onion, roughly
  chopped

1 bell pepper, any color, ribs and seeds
  removed and roughly chopped

1× 16-ounce (450g) package cubed ham,
  strained

4 tablespoons unsalted butter, divided

8–10 ounces (225-285g) frozen cubed
  potatoes, thawed

6 eggs

2 tablespoons everything bagel
  seasoning, divided

1× 10.5-ounce (298g) can cream of
  mushroom and garlic soup

½–1 cup shredded cheese of choice,
  plus extra for garnish

1 teaspoon salt

1 teaspoon freshly ground black pepper

1 teaspoon crushed red pepper flakes
  (reduce if sensitive to spice)

1 teaspoon ground cumin

1 batch store-bought or homemade
  biscuits, cut into quarters and placed
  in a bowl

1 teaspoon chopped fresh
  rosemary (optional)

Everything but the...
Biscuit Casserole

SERVES 6-8 | PREP TIME: 10 MINUTES | TOTAL TIME: 45 MINUTES

In the Midwest, we are famously known for casseroles, and in "church culture" after Mass, when we kids were finally free from restlessly wiggling our legs in a seated position throughout what felt like an endless service (which in actuality only lasted an hour), we were herded downstairs for a community breakfast. It didn't matter the occasion—rain or shine, one thing you could always count on seeing was the good ol' egg bake, a cross between breakfast casserole and the staple of breakfast—eggs! This was classically paired with a cold-cut sandwich on a dinner roll, breakfast sausage, Jell-O salad, a cookie, and optional juice or milk, or coffee for the adults.

I'm happy to introduce to you a Frankenstein's monster of two of my favorite things: breakfast and an egg bake hot dish. (Bonus: it's also great for meal prep.) *Can I get an "Amen"?* Cheesy, I know. Like this dish. I did it again. I'll see myself out.

1. Preheat the oven to 350°F (180°C).

2. In a medium saucepan over medium heat, add the olive oil, onion, and bell pepper, and cook for about 5 minutes. Add the ham, and cook for 5 more minutes. Transfer this mixture to a large casserole dish.

3. In the saucepan, melt 2 tablespoons butter. When the butter is melted, add the potatoes and cook for 5 minutes. Add the eggs, salt, pepper, red pepper flakes and cumin, with 1 tablespoon of everything bagel seasoning. Cook, scrambling the eggs, for about 5 minutes or until the potatoes and egg are starting to stick to the pan but they're mostly cooked. (Both will finish cooking in the oven.) (We're not seasoning this mixture with too much salt because there's plenty in the everything bagel seasoning.)

4. Add the cream of mushroom and garlic soup, the potato-egg mixture, and the cheese to the casserole dish, and mix thoroughly.

5. Top with additional cheese, if using. (I know I always do!)

6. Melt the remaining butter, and pour it over the biscuits. Add the rosemary, if using, and the remaining 1 tablespoon everything bagel seasoning, and toss the biscuits to coat. Layer the biscuits on top of the ingredients in the casserole dish, and bake for 35 to 45 minutes or until the biscuits start to turn golden brown and are cooked all the way through. They'll double in size for the most part, so that's how you'll know it's done!

7. Remove from the oven, and let it sit for 5 to 10 minutes before serving. Enjoy!

Double Bacon LTs

MAKES 4 INCREDIBLE SANDWICHES
PREP TIME: 10 MINUTES | TOTAL TIME: 35 MINUTES

This super simple recipe is something I like to think of as the ultimate BLT, like the Power Rangers morphing into a giant Megazord. Although this sandwich can be eaten at any time of day, it has proven extremely helpful for when I'm out on a hangry-induced farewell tour of mass destruction. It really checks all the boxes. I'm also very happy to admit I tested this recipe a few too many times, and it's still awesome.

I easily could have dubbed this the "Tacklebox BLT." I was first introduced to BLTs during the early Wisconsin mornings when Grandpa would get us ready to go fishing. We would have a feast of pancakes and BLTs before hopping into the old speedboat my grandpa captained around the lake. Have you ever had the "meat sweats" before? Because this sandwich is inspired by that feeling. Enjoy!

½ cup mayonnaise

3 tablespoons Dijon mustard

2 tablespoons sliced jarred sweet and spicy peppers (about 2 peppers if you like spice), plus 1 tablespoon brine

1 pound (450g) good quality bacon

½ tablespoon brown sugar (optional)

4 eggs (optional)

Sliced whole grain bread or something sturdy and thick, like Texas toast or a thick baguette

3–4 tablespoons unsalted butter

2 Roma tomatoes, cut into slices (about 4–6 slices)

Salt and freshly ground black pepper

1 head of iceberg lettuce, whole leaves removed (if you're here for the crunch), or arugula (if you're feeling fancy)

½ red onion, thinly sliced, or ¼ cup pickled onions

Pickle slices for the sandwiches or spears for serving

3 slices provolone or muenster

Special equipment

Baking rack

1. Preheat the oven to 350°F (180°C).

2. In a small bowl, combine the mayo, Dijon, sweet and spicy peppers, and pepper brine. Set aside, or pop it in the fridge until you're ready to assemble the sandwiches.

3. Arrange the bacon in a single layer on a rimmed baking sheet fitted with a baking rack, and bake for 15 to 20 minutes. Halfway through cook time, sprinkle some brown sugar, if using, over the bacon. You'll smell it when it's done. (This is also where snack bacon comes in handy. See Tips.) Remove from the oven, and transfer the bacon to a paper towel–lined plate.

4. Meanwhile, fry the eggs, if using, to your desired doneness.

5. Toast the bread using your preferred method (skillet or toaster). Then lightly butter the toast.

6. For assembly, you can stack this bad boy however you'd like. What I believe works best is one piece of toast, a hearty smear of the mayo, a layer of bacon (about 2 to 3 slices), a layer of tomato slices, and a little salt and pepper. Continue with the lettuce, red onion, pickle slices, the fried egg, if using, and then a slice of provolone. If the egg is still hot, it should perfectly melt the cheese. Smear the last piece of toast with more mayo, top the sandwich, and serve immediately. Enjoy!

.... **TIPS** ....

What is snack bacon, you ask? Snack bacon is the extra bacon you put in the oven along with the amount you planned on making so that when people get snoopy in the kitchen and aren't helping you cook, they can munch on the extra snack instead of stealing what you need to cook with. A pet peeve of mine is when people eat all the bacon and then there's not enough left for the intended purpose!

In this recipe, I like to jazz up some store-bought mayo by adding jarred peppers and a little brine, but you could just as easily swap in chopped pickles, a dash of vinegar, some minced garlic, and fresh herbs for an instant aioli. Or try a dash of hot sauce. A squeeze of fresh citrus works wonders with any of those flavor additions.

When you're finished with your jar of pickled peppers, don't you dare waste that delicious brine! Add some sliced onion to the jar, and whatever else you feel like pickling, and pop in the fridge to marinate overnight. You'll have delicious, low-effort pickles with tons of flavor.

APPETIZERS & FINGER FOODS

Pool Dip

SERVES 4-6 | PREP TIME: 10 MINUTES | TOTAL TIME: 10 MINUTES

Our Minnesota license plates used to say, "The land of 10,000 lakes," which is true, but we are also the land of 10,000 dips. You tell me which is more important? Spoiler alert: it's the lakes… but I do love the dips. I do not know anyone else in the world who takes "DIPS" as seriously as we Minnesotans do, and I'm here for it. As a Midwesterner who has to endure the gray and dull North Dakota winters, I thrive when I am lying poolside, tall, tan, handsome, and drinking a cocktail with this dip and a bowl of chips within reach. That's when I've reached my final form…happy!

1. In a medium bowl, combine the cream cheese, Greek yogurt, red pepper, and jalapeño until a somewhat smooth texture forms.

2. Add the black olives, corn, and black beans. Add the onion powder, garlic powder, parsley, dill, and dried chives, and stir until combined.

3. Add the lime juice and hot sauce, if using, and stir to incorporate.

4. You can serve this dip in the bowl you made it in or evenly distribute it in the bottom of a small casserole dish for easy serving. Garnish with green onions, fresh chives, or your choice of herb, and serve with tortilla and carrot chips. Enjoy!

1× 8-ounce (225g) block cream cheese, softened

½ cup Greek yogurt

1 red bell pepper, ribs removed and finely chopped or 6 ounces (170g) jarred roasted peppers, finely chopped

1 jalapeño or 3 ounces (85g) jarred jalapeños, minced or roughly chopped

1× 2-ounce (55g) can pitted black olives, drained and finely chopped

1× 15-ounce (425g) can corn, drained

1× 15-ounce (425g) can black beans, drained and rinsed

1 teaspoon onion powder

1 teaspoon garlic powder

1 teaspoon dried parsley

1 teaspoon dried dill

1 teaspoon dried chives

2 limes, juice of 1 and the other cut into wedges for garnish

Dash of hot sauce (I like Frank's RedHot sauce; optional)

3 green onions, or a handful of fresh chives or your choice herb, thinly sliced, for garnish

Serve with

Tortilla chips and carrot chips

1× 8-ounce (225g) block cream cheese, softened

¼ cup Homemade Ranch Dressing (see page 212) or store-bought

2 teaspoons sriracha or preferred hot sauce

3–4 dill pickles, roughly chopped

1 tablespoon minced garlic

½ bunch fresh dill, roughly chopped

5–6 jalapeños, cut horizontally like little bowls, seeds removed

10–12 strips bacon (about 1 pound/450g)

Special equipment

Toothpicks

> ·········· **TIP** ··········
>
> These can be cooked in an air fryer set to 370°F (187°C) for 10 to 12 minutes.

Jalapeño Pickle Poppers

MAKES 10-12 POPPERS | PREP TIME: 10 MINUTES | TOTAL TIME: 25 MINUTES

This is a marvelous creation I made for one of my best friends, Anna, a true "Pickle Girl" Midwest queen who's a little spicy but also one of the sweetest and most caring people I know. You might also appreciate her if you've tried some of my other pickle-y recipes—which are ALWAYS a hit—because she helps me come up with most of them. I draw a lot of inspiration from my friends and family, and this is a prime example. I hope you love and share it as much as she does.

1. Preheat the oven to 420°F (215°C).

2. In a small bowl, combine the cream cheese, Homemade Ranch Dressing, sriracha, dill pickles, garlic, and dill.

3. Evenly divide the pickle dip among the jalapeño "bowls." Wrap 1 slice of bacon around each filled jalapeño bowl, like a snake, and pin in place with a toothpick.

4. Arrange the bacon-wrapped jalapeños on a rimmed baking sheet fitted with a baking rack, and bake for about 12 to 15 minutes. After 12 minutes, check the bacon for doneness. It should be crispy.

5. Transfer the jalapeños to a plate, remove the toothpicks, and serve. Enjoy!

Pan-Fried Brie

SERVES 2-4 | PREP TIME: 5 MINUTES | TOTAL TIME: 25 MINUTES

I am no cheese snob—I'll get down with anything from Velveeta to the fanciest, stankiest bleu you could possibly find. It's all good with me. Brie is one of my favorite French cheeses because I love its soft, creamy, buttery taste. A lot of people are unsure about eating the rind, but I promise it's edible, and it adds a nice texture as well as a little bit of flavor to the cheese. I whip out this bad boy when I want to appear refined and like I have my life together—like I put a lot of thought into whatever I'm serving, when actually I threw together random ingredients I always have on hand (and everyone accidentally loved it anyway). I would make this for someone I was trying to impress, too. I love making this appetizer for all occasions, but especially if I'm on my third-date cooking vibes. (Just be sure to check beforehand if they have a sensitivity to lactose to prevent any awkward situations.)

3 tablespoons extra virgin olive oil

1 pint (10 ounces/285g) cherry tomatoes

Good pinch of kosher salt

1× 8-ounce (225g) wheel Brie (any level of cream), the top scored to create a checkered pattern

2–4 garlic cloves, minced

4–5 sliced figs

Handful of fresh basil leaves, for garnish

Balsamic glaze, for garnish

1 loaf of crusty bread or 1 baguette, cut into bite-sized pieces

---

TIP

You can bake this in the oven instead of cooking it on the stove if you have limited room. Add everything to an oven-safe pan and bake at 350°F (180°C) for 15 to 20 minutes. If you have a lid for your baking dish, great. If not it, will still be delicious uncovered in the oven.

---

1. In a cast-iron skillet or a medium pan over medium-low heat, add the extra virgin olive oil, cherry tomatoes, and salt, and cook for about 5 to 8 minutes or until the tomatoes are blistered.

2. Make a well in the center of the tomatoes large enough for the Brie wheel to fit, and add the Brie to the pan.

3. Spread the garlic over the top of the Brie, getting it into all the cuts, and then top with the figs.

4. Cover the pan, reduce the heat to low, and cook for 10 to 15 minutes or the Brie is hot and super melty.

5. Top with the basil and drizzle the balsamic glaze over the all. Serve immediately from the pan alongside the bread. Enjoy!

Mexican-Inspired Queso

SERVES 4–6 AS AN APPETIZER | PREP TIME: 5 MINUTES
TOTAL TIME: 25 MINUTES

Consider this ANOTHER cheese-appreciation recipe, and welcome to my TED Talk about cheese and the reasons I love it. Cheese comes from all around the world, but I'm especially fond of Wisconsin cheese, in part because Wisconsinites call themselves the "cheese heads" and I love imagining people walking around with big chunks of cheddar in place of their heads! Nevertheless, it's all good where I'm from! Cheese—we know her, we love her. She works in both savory and sweet applications; contains protein (so, practically a health food); and is portable in slices, sticks, or cans. Cheese can be made into snacks, main dishes, and desserts, and it's hard to ruin—if you cook it until it's extra crispy, it's still good! Cheese pulls; enough said. I love cheese, and this dish is only a highlight of one of the many ways I love to eat it. This recipe can be made with Velveeta, and that's totally fine, but I recommend using queso Oaxaca if you can find it!

1 pound (450g) chorizo (any kind)

1× 10-ounce (285g) block queso Oaxaca or Velveeta (or a mix of both), roughly torn or cut into 1-inch (2.5cm) pieces

4 ounces (115g) cream cheese (about ½ a block), cut into 1-inch (2.5cm) cubes

2 bell peppers (any color), ribs and seeds removed and roughly chopped

1 white or yellow onion, roughly chopped, plus extra for garnish (optional)

¼ cup pickled jalapeños, plus extra for garnish (optional)

1× 10-ounce (285g) can diced tomatoes with green chilies

Fresh cilantro, jarred or homemade salsa, or crema (table cream), for garnish

Serve with

Tortilla chips and/or warm tortillas

1. Preheat the oven to 350°F (180°C).

2. In an oven-safe pan over medium heat, cook the chorizo for about 8 to 10 minutes, or until browned. Transfer to a plate.

3. Evenly distribute the queso Oaxaca in the bottom of the pan, followed by cream cheese, bell peppers, onion, and the jalapeños, if using, and the canned tomatoes. Mix until combined then add the chorizo to the pan, on top of the cheese and bake for 15 minutes or until the cheese is melted and bubbling.

4. Remove from the oven. Top with more pickled jalapeños and onions, if using, cilantro, salsa, crema, or your favorite garnishes, and serve immediately with tortilla chips and/or warm tortillas. Enjoy!

Homemade Shrimp Cocktail

SERVES 6-10 | PREP TIME: 10 MINUTES | TOTAL TIME: 30 MINUTES

1 white or yellow onion, cut into quarters

2 carrots, roughly chopped

2 celery stalks, roughly chopped

1 shallot, cut in half

1 head of garlic, horizontally sliced

2 lemons, 1 cut in half for the shrimp and 1 cut into wedges, for garnish

½ bunch fresh thyme (about 5-6 sprigs)

3 sprigs of rosemary

2 fresh or dried bay leaves

1-2 pounds (450g-1kg) raw shrimp, peeled and deveined, fully thawed if frozen

For the cocktail sauce

1 cup ketchup

Zest of ½ lemon

½ tablespoon prepared horseradish

1 teaspoon rice wine vinegar

1 teaspoon Worcestershire sauce

1 teaspoon hot sauce of choice (optional, but recommended)

> ·········· **TIP** ··········
>
> After the shrimp are done cooking, save the stock. Strain out the vegetables and herbs, and use it to make Blender Lobster Bisque (see page 198)!

There was a point, as I was growing up, when my great-grandma came to live with us. This is something special that I didn't really appreciate at the time. I remember Grandma Pauley as being very sweet. She and her husband fostered so many kids when they lived on their farm in Wisconsin. She introduced us to a lot of my favorite Polish and Norwegian foods, which I also didn't always appreciate at the time as much as I do now. This is also when Grandma insisted that we start eating shrimp with homemade cocktail sauce whenever we pulled out a meat and cheese board on holidays. This recipe will blow away the frozen kits you buy at the store. Now you, too, can witness the magic that is horseradish and its ability to clear any sinuses!

1. To a large pot add the onion, carrots, celery, shallot, garlic, 1 lemon, thyme, rosemary, bay leaves, and 1 quart (1 liter) water and bring to a boil over high heat. Add the shrimp, and cook, stirring occasionally, for 5 to 8 minutes or until the shrimp turns a beautiful red-pink color. Remove the shrimp from the broth and veggies, and transfer to a bowl with ice water to chill, or on a clean plate in the fridge until ready to serve.

2. Combine all the cocktail sauce ingredients in a small to medium bowl.

3. To serve, line a plate with crushed ice, assemble the shrimp on top of the ice, and serve with the cocktail sauce and some lemon wedges. Enjoy!

4 tablespoons unsalted butter, at room
   temperature

½ cup hot sauce (I use Frank's RedHot)

2 tablespoons olive oil

½ cup sour cream

1 teaspoon ground cumin

2 teaspoons garlic powder

2 teaspoons onion powder

1 teaspoon Cajun seasoning, or to taste

1 teaspoon dried parsley

1 teaspoon dried dill

1 teaspoon dried chives, plus extra for
   garnish (optional)

2½–3 pounds (1.25–1.5kg) chicken wings/
   drumsticks, fresh or frozen

Grated Parmesan, for garnish (optional)

Fresh parsley, for garnish (optional)

Serve with

Homemade Ranch Dressing (page 212)
   or bleu cheese dressing

Special equipment

Meat thermometer

············ **TIP** ············

If you like your sauce
extra spicy, add small
amounts of cayenne
pepper to the sauce—
about ¼ teaspoon at a
time—as you're making
it and taste as you go.

Dive Bar Buffalo Wings

SERVES 4–6 | PREP TIME: 5 MINUTES | TOTAL TIME: 50 MINUTES

This is a recipe based on one of my all-time favorite wing places, which was featured on *Diners, Drive-Ins and Dives*—The Parrot's Cay! It's a staple here in Grand Forks and is where everyone goes to watch the UND (University of North Dakota) hockey games. It's a dive bar where everything is served on paper plates and the walls are covered with knick-knacks and handwritten graffiti that's all fascinating to look at. It's a damn good time full of hometown pride. Be sure to have some paper towels nearby because your hands get completely covered in the sauce, and I mean that in the best way. Messy eaters are welcome! Serve these wings with a side of ranch or bleu cheese dressing, some fries or tater tots, and an ice-cold beverage.

1. Preheat the oven to 400°F (200°C).

2. Line a baking sheet with foil for easy cleanup, and place a baking rack on the foil. Lightly coat the rack with cooking spray so the chicken won't stick to it.

3. In a large bowl, combine the butter, hot sauce, olive oil, and sour cream. Add the cumin, garlic powder, onion powder, Cajun seasoning, parsley, dill, and chives, and mix until combined.

4. Add half of the sauce to a separate bowl, and set aside. Add the chicken wings to the remaining sauce in the large bowl, and toss using tongs until the wings are completely coated.

5. Arrange the chicken on the prepared rack, and bake for up to 45 minutes, depending on how large the wings are, checking for doneness at 35 minutes. Remove from the oven when the chicken is fully cooked and has reached an internal temperature of 165°F (75°C).

6. Add the cooked wings to the bowl of remaining sauce, give them another toss for even more sauce, and arrange on a plate. Garnish with Parmesan and chives or parsley, if using, and serve immediately with Homemade Ranch Dressing or bleu cheese dressing for dipping. Enjoy!

Strawberry-Ricotta Crostini

SERVES 6–10 | PREP TIME: 5 MINUTES
TOTAL TIME: 20 MINUTES

This was an appetizer I loved serving when I was doing some light catering jobs and getting started in the food industry. Everyone loves it because it's an easy, delicious, and refreshing bite any time of year. It's also very easily customizable. You can easily replace the strawberries with whatever fruit you want. I especially love making it during stone fruit season, and I highly recommend subbing peaches, plums, or nectarines for the strawberries when you can. If you're looking to throw together a meat and cheese board or some fruit dip, these crostini are a great accompaniment.

1 baguette, cut into 1-inch (2.5cm) slices

3 tablespoons extra virgin olive oil or softened unsalted butter

1 cup ricotta (any fat percentage)

4 ounces (115g) cream cheese (about ½ a block)

1 teaspoon poppy seeds (optional)

3 tablespoons honey, plus extra for garnish

Zest and juice of ½ lemon

1 pint (475g) fresh strawberries, tops removed and sliced

1 cup pistachios, walnuts, or nuts of choice (optional)

Drizzle of hot honey, for garnish

Handful of fresh basil or mint, for garnish

Special equipment

Food processor

1. Preheat the oven to 350°F (180°C).

2. Place the baguette slices on a baking sheet, drizzle with olive oil (or spread butter) on one side, and toast in the oven for 10 to 15 minutes.

3. Meanwhile, in a food processor, whip together the ricotta, cream cheese, poppy seeds (if using), honey, and lemon.

4. To the toasted bread, add a spoonful of the whipped cheese mixture followed by some sliced strawberries. Sprinkle with nuts, if using, and drizzle with honey or hot honey. Garnish with little sprigs of fresh basil or mint, and serve. Enjoy!

1× 8-ounce (245g) roll puff pastry

1-2 beefsteak tomatoes, thinly sliced

1 teaspoon salt and freshly ground black
pepper

1 cup ricotta (any fat percentage)

2-3 garlic cloves

2 tablespoons extra virgin olive oil

Handful of colorful cherry tomatoes,
thinly sliced

Pinch of flaky salt

2× 4-ounce (115g) balls burrata or fresh
mozzarella

Pinch of Italian seasoning

Handful of fresh basil, torn

2 tablespoons fresh or dried chives,
chopped

Special equipment

Food processor

> **......... TIP ....**
>
> Poking the puff pastry
> with a fork, called
> docking, creates
> ventilation holes for
> steam to escape as the
> pastry bakes. This is key
> to avoiding a soggy
> bottom!

Tomato Galette

SERVES 4 | PREP TIME: 5 MINUTES | TOTAL TIME: 30 MINUTES

I'm going to paint a picture for you: in another life, I'm picking fresh tomatoes in a bountiful garden that's attached to a refurbished lighthouse in the French countryside where I live with my darling husband, who has long eyelashes, a sexy foreign accent, and looks like a Hemsworth brother; and he and I are going to bake these galettes in our rustic kitchen. It's my dream! However, I'm in THIS reality...which is still cool...and...great... and fun sometimes. Anyway, the galette IS real in this life, so I'll take what I can get! And I'll share it with you instead.

1. Preheat the oven to 350°F (180°C). Line a baking sheet with parchment paper for easy cleanup.

2. Roll out the puff pastry, cut it into 4 squares, and place them on the prepared baking sheet 1 inch (2.5cm). Using a fork, poke holes all over the pastry squares 1 inch (2.5cm) apart.

3. Place the beefsteak tomato slices on a plate, and season with a healthy pinch of salt. This will help them release some extra juices.

4. In a food processor, blend the ricotta, garlic, extra virgin olive oil, salt, and pepper for about 2 or 3 minutes or until light and fluffy (like a Cool Whip texture).

5. Spread the whipped ricotta on the puff pastry, and assemble the beefsteak tomato slices and the cherry tomatoes on top in whatever pattern you'd like. Bake for 25 minutes or until the crust is beautifully golden brown.

6. Top with flaky salt and torn pieces of burrata, and sprinkle with Italian seasoning, basil, and/or chives, and serve. Enjoy!

Sausage & Sauerkraut Flatbread

SERVES 4–6 AS AN APPETIZER OR 2–4 AS A MAIN
PREP TIME: 10 MINUTES | TOTAL TIME: 50 MINUTES

My love for sauerkraut started with my grandma, who sends us jars of her canning creations as gifts for holidays along with lovely baked goods (in a cute round tin, of course). I like to serve it with smoked sausage because I was that weird kid at the barbecue who wanted a mountain of pickles, sauerkraut, and mustard on his plate while all the other kids were loading up on whipped cookie salad. Now that I'm an adult and DGAF about what anyone says, I enjoy it as much as I can. And there are good probiotics in sauerkraut as well, which makes it even neater!

Cooking spray, for greasing (optional)

2 tablespoons unsalted butter

1× 14-ounce (115g) can sauerkraut, drained

2–3 tablespoons all-purpose flour, for dusting

1 pound (450g) Homemade Pizza Dough (see page 210) or store-bought (I like to use a whole wheat dough for this)

1 tablespoon coarse-ground mustard

1 teaspoon freshly prepared horseradish

3–4 garlic cloves, minced

2 tablespoons olive oil

6–8 ounces (170–225g) freshly grated Gruyère or cheddar, or an equal mix of both

2–3 precooked smoked sausage links, cut into 1-inch (2.5cm) coins

3–4 sprigs of thyme, stems removed

1. Preheat the oven to 350°F (180°C). Lightly coat a baking sheet (if using) with cooking spray. Or make sure you have enough flour on the bottom of your pizza to easily remove from the pan.

2. In a medium pan over low to medium heat, melt the butter. When the butter has melted, add the drained sauerkraut, and cook for 8 to 10 minutes or until most of the liquid has evaporated. Transfer the sauerkraut to a plate, and set aside.

3. Lightly flour your work surface, and use a rolling pin to roll out the Homemade Pizza Dough to fit the baking sheet you're using. Gently transfer the dough to the prepared baking sheet.

4. In a small bowl, mix together the coarse-ground mustard, horseradish, garlic, and olive oil. Evenly brush the oil mixture over the crust.

5. Spread an even layer of Gruyère over the oil mixture and then top with the sausage coins and sauerkraut and top with fresh thyme .

6. Bake for 25 to 30 minutes or until the crust has started to turn golden.

7. Remove from the oven and let cool for a few minutes on the baking sheet. Cut into slices and serve. Enjoy!

> ·········· **TIP** ··········
>
> My Homemade Pizza Dough recipe (see page 210) calls for all-purpose flour, and it works great, but you totally could substitute 1 cup of the flour called for with whole wheat flour for a great-tasting crust.

Chocolate Chip Cannoli Dip

SERVES 4–6 | PREP TIME: 5 MINUTES
TOTAL TIME: 10 MINUTES

1 cup ricotta (any fat percentage)

1× 8-ounce (225g) package mascarpone or cream cheese, softened

1 cup confectioners' sugar

1 teaspoon vanilla extract

½ cup mini chocolate chips or mini chocolate-covered candy (such as M&M's)

1× 7-ounce (200g) box waffle cone bowls, keep 1 or 2 bowls whole and the break the rest into bite-sized pieces

Special equipment

Electric hand mixer

I originally wanted to make some really cute cannoli because apparently I'm very Italian, according to Ancestry.com. Unfortunately, every time I tried to order cannoli shells online, they always arrived broken and unsalvageable. This sparked a thought: If this keeps happening to me, it's going to happen to someone else, and I wouldn't want this to happen to someone else who wants to make this recipe. And then I was like, Duhhh. Keep it simple, stupid. Use ingredients that people would more likely be able to find! Bada bing, bada boom. Here is a stupid-easy dessert appetizer that's inspired by my love of a good cannoli and newfound Italian heritage.

··········· **TIP** ···········

This recipe makes enough of the ricotta filling for two waffle cone bowls—one to serve and one for a refill later (or one for taste-testing if you know what I mean). You can make the filling beforehand and chill it until ready to serve.

1. In a large bowl, add the ricotta, mascarpone, confectioners' sugar, and vanilla extract. Give it a rough mix with a rubber spatula or whisk so things don't splash out before switching to an electric mixer on high and blending until smooth.

2. Fold in the chocolate chips until evenly distributed.

3. Fill the whole waffle bowls with some of the ricotta mix, and serve with the bite-sized pieces for scooping (like a potato chip situation) . Enjoy!

Nutty Cheese Logs & Meat Board

LOG SERVES 4–8; FULL BOARD FEEDS A CROWD OF 8–10
PREP TIME: 5 MINUTES | TOTAL TIME: 10 MINUTES

This is a really delicious recipe that everyone—I repeat, EVERYONE—who tries it will love. It's so stupidly easy and requires no cooking whatsoever. My love for meat and cheese trays goes back to when I was a kid, when my mom would make them. I loved making little cracker sandwiches—spreading on dips followed by meats and cheese and finished with an olive—and would often eat too many before dinner was served. I also love how these types of spreads have been repackaged or rebranded and offered to children (aka Lunchables). These types of boards make an appearance at all my get-togethers.

1. In a medium bowl, combine the olive oil, if using, chives, parsley, basil, rosemary, oregano, garlic powder, lemon zest, nuts, and crushed red pepper flakes, if using.

2. Pour half of the seasonings mixture onto a length of plastic wrap or a reusable parchment or silicone mat, and spread into an even layer.

3. Roll 1 log of goat cheese log in the seasonings, tightly pressing it as you roll so the seasonings embed into the cheese. Or you can arrange the nuts in a cute pattern if you'd like. If using plastic wrap, you can roll and seal the cheese log in the plastic until you're ready to serve or transport. Repeat the process with remaining herbs and cheese log.

4. Arrange the cheese logs on your board with a variety of crackers/bread, nuts, fruits, other cheeses, charcuterie, and jams, and serve. Enjoy!

For the cheese logs

2 tablespoons extra virgin olive oil (optional)

2 teaspoons chopped fresh chives

2 teaspoons chopped fresh parsley

2 teaspoons fresh basil

1 teaspoon dried rosemary

1 teaspoon dried oregano

1 teaspoon garlic powder

Zest of ½ lemon

½ cup nut of choice, chopped (I like to use sliced almonds or substitute french fried onions, crushed)

1 teaspoon crushed red pepper flakes (optional)

2× 8-ounce (225g) goat cheese logs (I recommend plain goat cheese)

For the full board

Variety of crackers and/or bread (I recommend a toasted sourdough), nuts, fresh and/or dried fruits, other cheeses, charcuterie, and jams

---

TIPS

A styling trick that I like to use when arranging things on a single board is making a rainbow or ombre pattern—1. because everyone knows what a rainbow is, so it's pretty identifiable, and 2. because I love rainbows!

Give yourself a little extra time to prepare this board if you enjoy styling a plate. It's therapeutic and a great way to release some creative energy!

HANDHELDS

Grilled Pear & Prosciutto Melts

SERVES 2-4 | PREP TIME: 5 MINUTES | TOTAL TIME: 20 MINUTES

This recipe is inspired by one of my favorite date spots in my hometown, Ely's Ivy. I like it because it's unique, uses local produce and large game, and is very farm-to-table with a good atmosphere and big windows. This light, refreshing sandwich is usually what I order when I'm there, grilling my date with questions. I like to judge my date's mood based on what they order at a restaurant—do they want to share food? Are they as cute as their online profile? And of, course, are they funny? All indicators I look for when falling in love with a human or a sandwich.

4 tablespoons unsalted butter or mayonnaise

4 slices sourdough or bread of choice

1× 8-ounce (226g) wheel Brie, rind removed, cut into ½-inch (1.25cm) slices

6 ounces (170g) prosciutto

2 pears, thinly sliced

9 ounces (255g) canned artichoke halves, drained

1 ounce (30g) homemade or store-bought pickled red onions per sandwich (optional)

Handful of arugula (optional)

Balsamic glaze, for drizzling

1. Butter one side of each piece of bread, and place two pieces buttered side down on a plate. Add half of the Brie to each piece of bread, followed by half of the prosciutto, sliced pear, artichokes, pickled red onions (if using), arugula (if using), and balsamic glaze. Top with the remaining slices of bread, butter sides up.

2. In a large skillet over low to medium heat, cook the sandwiches for 5 to 7 minutes or until golden brown. Flip over the sandwiches, and cook for 5 to 7 minutes more or until golden brown. When you can see the cheese starting to melt over the side of the sandwiches, they're done.

3. Transfer the sandwiches to a plate, cut, and serve. Enjoy!

TIPS

You don't want the heat to be too high because you're essentially making grilled cheese. Low and slow is the way to go.

If you haven't tried making grilled cheese using mayo instead of butter, please try it. I prefer it. Mayo has a similar flavor, is super spreadable, and toasts the bread to a wonderfully crisp gold brown.

Mom's Steak Bite Sandwiches au Jus

SERVES 6-8 | PREP TIME: 30 MINUTES | TOTAL TIME: 1 HOUR 25 MINUTES

Whenever we asked my mom, "What's for dinner?" and her response was, "Steak bite sandwiches," my siblings and I would cheer and run off to enjoy our good fortune. This is one of those recipes that would test our patience because we could smell it cooking throughout the house. We'd be kind of like those cartoon animals being carried away by a smell. It's intoxicating. You can dress this up and make it all fancy, or you can make it extremely quickly with a tube of store-bought dough. Don't expect there to be any leftovers.

Sprinkle of all-purpose flour, for dusting

1 pound (450g) Homemade Pizza Dough (see page 210) or store-bought pizza dough

4 tablespoons unsalted butter

½ red or white onion, thinly sliced

1 celery stalk, thinly sliced

6 ounces (170g) portobello mushrooms, thinly sliced

4–6 garlic cloves, minced

1½ pounds (680g) sirloin tips, cut into 1-inch (2.5cm) cubes (you also could use venison)

Salt and freshly ground black pepper

1 tablespoon fresh or dried oregano

1¼ cups shredded mozzarella or Swiss cheese

¼ cup grated Parmesan

1 large egg

2 cups beef broth

> **········· TIP ·········**
>
> Do not forget to make those slashes in the dough, or you are not going to be pleased with the resulting soggy sandwich!

1. Preheat the oven to 375°F (190°C). Line an 11×13-inch (28×33cm) baking sheet with parchment paper.

2. Lightly flour your work surface, and use a rolling pin to roll out the pizza dough to fit the baking sheet you're using. Gently transfer the dough to the baking sheet.

3. In a large pan over medium heat, melt 3 tablespoons of the butter then add the onion, celery, mushrooms, and about ¾ of the garlic for 8 to 10 minutes.

4. Add the sirloin tips, salt, pepper, and oregano to the pan, and cook for 6 to 8 minutes or until the meat reaches your desired doneness. (My preference is pink but not red.) Remove from the heat, transfer the steak mixture to a plate, and reserve the liquid from the pan in a glass measuring cup.

5. Sprinkle half mozzarella and Parmesan evenly over the pizza dough and then distribute the steak mixture over the top. Sprinkle on the remaining cheese; it will work as a sealant so the meat mixture doesn't get soggy. Grab the dough side closest to you and roll it onto itself, folding the edges under the rolled portion. Pinch the dough together to seal all sides if needed and then roll it lightly to form a log. The goal is not to

allow any meat or other goodness to poke through the dough; otherwise, you're going to have a soggy bottom on your hands. You also don't want to roll this too many times because you don't want it to be doughy. Place the log seam-side down on the baking sheet, and cut four small 1-inch (2.5cm) slashes into the top, just like you would a loaf of bread.

6. In a small bowl, whisk together the egg and a splash of water. Brush the egg wash over the log to seal the deal, and bake for 25 to 30 minutes. When it's ready, the log will be lovely golden brown on top.

7. Remove from the oven, and set aside to cool while you make the sauce. (Don't cut it yet. Wait until it's cooled.)

8. Return the juices from the meat mixture to the pan with the remaining butter, the beef broth, and the remaining garlic if desired. The "jus" is supposed to be a loose liquid dip, but if you want to thicken it up, add a little all-purpose flour to the mix.

9. Cut the cooled log into slices for serving, and serve alongside the "jus" for dipping like a French dip or like a gravy for your handheld masterpiece! Enjoy!

Friendsgiving Melts with Cranberry Sauce

SERVES 2-4 | PREP TIME: 5 MINUTES | TOTAL TIME: 20 MINUTES

I low-key make this sandwich or wrap just for the cranberry sauce. Cranberry sauce is usually my favorite part of Thanksgiving, besides the mashed potatoes. My obsession with cranberries is part of my family legacy—we own a cranberry marsh in Wisconsin. We have cranberry juice running through our veins. If you've seen *Friends*, you might refer to this as a "moistmaker," and I promise I won't make a stink if you eat my leftover sandwich because holy crapola, it's sensational. Enjoy this year round or utilize leftovers. Regardless, happy holidays!

1. Preheat the oven to 350°F (180°C).

2. Place the hoagie rolls cut side up on a baking sheet. Spread the goat cheese on one side of each roll. On the other side, assemble a layer of turkey, prosciutto, and Brie slices.

3. Bake, open faced, for 10 to 15 minutes or until the cheeses are warm and melty.

4. Meanwhile, warm the gravy in a small pan over medium-low heat.

5. When the sandwich is finished toasting, remove from the oven. Add a layer of gravy to the cheese and meat side, crumble some potato chips over the gravy, and add a few apple slices on top. Place the goat cheese side of the roll over the other side to make a sandwich, and serve. (Rest assured, barely anything falls out of the sandwich with this structure. It's lovely, and I hope you enjoy it because you're also lovely.)

2 hoagie rolls, cut horizontally

4 ounces (115g) cranberry goat cheese, divided

8 ounces (225g) turkey slices or rotisserie chicken, divided

3 ounces (85g) prosciutto or smoked or honey ham, divided

4 ounces (115g) Brie or camembert, cut into thin slices, divided

4 ounces (115g) homemade or store-bought gravy (anything works, but I like beef gravy)

Handful of potato chips or store-bought french fried onions

1 Granny Smith apple, cored and cut into thin slices

3 tablespoons Krell/Haas Family Cranberry Sauce (recipe to follow)

Krell/Haas Family Cranberry Sauce

1. In a medium or large pan over medium heat, combine all of the ingredients. Bring to a simmer and then begin stirring frequently to ensure nothing sticks to the bottom of the pan.

2. After about 10 minutes, put on some oven mitts, possibly ones you dont care about getting a little dirty, and use the back of a wooden spoon to pop most of the cranberries. Continue to cook, stirring, for 10 more minutes. Remove from the heat and let the mixture cool.

3. Serve the sauce at room temperature. Store any leftovers in an airtight container in the refrigerator for up to 2 weeks.

For cranberry sauce

18 ounces (510g) fresh cranberries

1 cup water

1 cup orange juice (fresh is best when possible!)

¾–1 cup lightly packed brown sugar

½ cup granulated sugar

Zest of ½ orange

2 cinnamon sticks

Pinch of nutmeg

1 whole star anise (optional)

Pinch of ground allspice

Splash of vanilla extract (optional, but seriously, add it!)

½ cup Kewpie mayonnaise

5 tablespoons jarred sweet and spicy peppers, minced

2–3 garlic cloves, minced

1 loaf ciabatta bread or 1 baguette, cut horizontally

4 ounces (115g) prosciutto, sliced

4 ounces (115g) peppered salami, sliced

3 ounces (85g) capicola, sliced

6–8 ounces (170–225g) fresh mozzarella, sliced

5 tablespoons Delishaas Pesto (see page 127) or store-bought pesto

2–3 ounces (55–85g) mixed greens or spinach

6–8 banana peppers, sliced

Handful of fresh basil

Drizzle of red wine vinegar

Drizzle of extra virgin olive oil

Few sprinkles of dried oregano

Italian Heroes

SERVES 2 (OR 1 VERY HUNGRY PERSON) | PREP TIME: 5 MINUTES
TOTAL TIME: 20 MINUTES

There was a time when the #9 Italian Night Club Sandwich from Jimmy John's was my absolute obsession. I would eat it every day for lunch, and it was my drunk delivery order (when I wasn't craving pizza). I loved that this sandwich had such an alluring and unconventional name, and it was the best "Italian meats" that were affordable and available to me at the time. Eventually, I figured out how to make it at home—and make it 10 times better. If you're making this for lunch to bring to work, you are going to make everyone else so jealous.

1. Preheat the oven to 350°F (180°C).

2. In a small bowl, combine the mayonnaise, sweet and spicy peppers, and garlic. Set aside.

3. Place the ciabatta cut side up on a baking sheet. On the bottom layer of the bread, add a layer of prosciutto, peppered salami, and capicola. Top with slices of mozzarella, and toast in the oven for about 10 minutes or until the cheese is melty.

4. Remove from the oven and spread on a layer of Delishaas Pesto. Top with some mixed greens, banana peppers, and fresh basil.

5. When you're ready to eat, drizzle the sandwich with red wine vinegar and extra virgin olive oil and sprinkle a little oregano over the top. (If you're making this for a picnic or something ahead of time, don't add the vinegar and oil until ready to serve.)

6. Spread some mayo on the top layer of the bread, and press on the meat side to make a sandwich. Cut into however many pieces you like, and serve immediately with your favorite crunchy chip situation. Enjoy!

Grandma Geneva's Fish Tacos with Lefsen

SERVES 16–20 MINI TACOS | PREP TIME: 30 MINUTES
TOTAL TIME: 1 HOUR 30 MINUTES (PLUS 1 HOUR RESTING TIME)

I have the fondest memories of the times at my grandma's lake cabin when she would let me join her in the kitchen. She's famous for her family-sized meals, especially these fish tacos. They are the perfect blend of crunchy, tangy, and sour with a little spice all wrapped into a bite-sized moment, and this is the ideal dish to showcase Grandma's talent for the perfect fish fry. The fresh lefsen are treated like tortillas, but because they're made from potatoes, they're subtly soft and chewy. I don't think I've cleaned and gutted a fish since I was a kid (that job was for Grandpa John), and if you watched my *Chopped* episode, you'll see that I handed off that job to my co-cooking partner. Luckily, this dish is easy to do with fillets, but if you do happen to have some fresh fish from the lake, it's party time.

To make the lefsen

1. In a small pan over medium-high heat, bring 1¼ cup water to a boil. Add the salt and butter. When the butter has melted into the water, remove from the heat.

2. In a large bowl, combine the instant mashed potatoes, flour, and butter-water mixture stirring until smooth.

3. In the same small pan over low heat, whisk together the shortening and buttermilk until the mixture is smooth and warm but not scorching. Pour into the bowl with the flour mixture, and stir until a smooth dough forms. Cover the bowl with a clean towel and let the dough rest for 1 hour in the fridge.

4. Use the remaining flour to dust your work surface. Remove the dough from the refrigerator and begin rolling into balls the size of the circle created by touching the tip of your index finger to the tip of your thumb. Roll the dough into as many balls as you'd like; this recipe makes about 16 to 20 balls. Next, use a rolling pin or clean wine bottle to roll the balls into thin disks, each 6 or 7 inches (15–17.75cm) in diameter. Stack the disks between pieces of wax or parchment paper until ready to cook.

5. In a skillet or nonstick pan over high heat, cook the lefsen in batches (do not crowd the pan) for 1 or 2 minutes per side until beautiful brown spots appear. Transfer the lefsen to a linen- or parchment paper–lined plate and repeat with the remaining disks.

To make the fish tacos

1. Begin by making the batter. To a medium bowl, add 1 cup flour, and set aside.

2. In a separate medium bowl, whisk together the remaining 1 cup flour, onion powder, garlic powder, paprika, salt, and pepper. Pour in the beer, and whisk again to combine.

3. In a large, deep pan over medium-high heat, heat the vegetable oil to 350°F (180°C).

4. Dredge each whitefish fillet in the reserved 1 cup of flour, one at a time, and then dip in the beer batter until fully coated, removing any excess.

5. Working in batches, fry the fish in the hot oil for about 2 minutes per side. The fillet should be golden brown on both sides before removing. Transfer the cooked fillets to a paper towel–lined plate to drain, and repeat with the remaining fillets.

6. For the sauce, combine the mayonnaise, Greek yogurt, shallot, lime juice, and half of the chopped cilantro in a small bowl.

7. To assemble the tacos, smear a spoonful of the sauce on the inside of one lefse and then add some fried fish, coleslaw, pickled onions, more cilantro, if using, and a dash of hot sauce. Serve with lime wedges. Enjoy!

For the lefsen

1 teaspoon kosher salt

2 tablespoons unsalted butter, softened

3 cups instant mashed potatoes

1 cup all-purpose flour, plus more for
dusting

2 tablespoons shortening

¾ cup buttermilk or milk of choice

For the fish tacos

2 cups all-purpose flour, divided

1 teaspoon onion powder

1 teaspoon garlic powder

1 teaspoon sweet paprika

Salt and freshly ground black pepper

1 × 8-ounce can beer such as Budweiser
(my grandma's favorite)

2 cups vegetable or canola oil, for frying

3 pounds (1.5kg) whitefish fillets of
choice (my family uses walleye),
patted dry

½ cup mayonnaise

½ cup Greek yogurt

1 shallot, minced

2 limes, 1 juiced and 1 cut into slices, for
serving

1 bunch fresh cilantro or parsley,
roughly chopped, divided

1 × 8-ounce (225g) bag pre-cut coleslaw
mix

Pickled red onions

Dash of hot sauce of choice

Special equipment

Rolling pin

Wax or parchment paper, cut into
6-inch (17cm) squares

Thermometer

For the dough

1½ cups all-purpose flour, plus extra for dusting

2 teaspoons baking powder

Heavy pinch of salt (a heaping ¼ teaspoon)

¾ cup whole milk or water

2 cups vegetable or canola oil, for frying (you may need more or less depending on the depth your pan)

For the filling

1 pound (450g) ground beef or ground protein of choice (any fat percentage)

1 white or yellow onion, finely chopped, divided

4 garlic cloves, minced

2 teaspoons Italian seasoning

2 teaspoons chili powder

2 teaspoons smoked paprika

1 teaspoon ground cumin

Salt and freshly ground black pepper

For the toppings

Shredded lettuce (I like iceberg for the crunch)

Diced tomatoes or salsa

Sliced black olives

Sliced jalapeños

Sour cream

Chopped fresh cilantro or sliced green onions

Shredded cheese of choice

Special equipment

Rolling pin

Thermometer

········· **TIP** ·········

This dough also can be used as a dessert. When tossed in sugar and cinnamon, it's reminiscent of a churro! Or try dipping it in a sweetened cream cheese dip; it's truly lovely!

Fry Bread Tacos (Navajo Tacos)

SERVES 6–8 | PREP TIME: 15 MINUTES | TOTAL TIME: 45 MINUTES

I was introduced to this dish at my Grandma Geneva's house in the upper Midwest, where they are sometimes called oofda tacos. This recipe has its roots in an Indigenous dish known as fry bread tacos or Navajo tacos. This was a dish that was created out of necessity; as the Indigenous people were forced onto reservations and their resources became more limited, these were some of the only ingredients that were available to them so they found a way to turn that struggle into something delicious. I am Ojibwe by blood, and although my family and I aren't practicing Indigenous people, I believe it's important to learn from our history. I do not care if we are talking about race, gender, sexuality, equality, or any topic in between. We are the people who are writing history now, and I believe that we all should be treated equally and not repeat the cycles of past oppression. Learning from our past and sharing recipes that bring people together and tell the sometimes difficult stories of our history is just one of the ways to start changing the narrative. Let's change the world by bringing people together with food.

1. Begin by making the dough. In a medium or large bowl, lightly whisk together the all-purpose flour, baking powder, and salt. Add the milk, and stir until just combined, being sure not to overmix, it might be kind of lumpy, but it will hydrate. Cover and set aside to rest for 15 minutes while you prep the toppings.

2. When the dough is ready, turn it out onto a lightly floured surface, and divide it into 6 to 8 equal-size balls. Use a rolling pin to roll out the balls into disks each about 4 or 5 inches (10–12.5cm) in diameter. Make a small hole about ½ inch (1.25cm) in the center of each disk if you want it to fry a little flatter. (It will fill in for the most part when frying.)

3. In a large cast-iron or high-sided pan over medium-high heat, heat the vegetable oil to 350°F (180°C).

4. Working in batches depending on the size of the pan you're using, fry the disks for 3 or 4 minutes per side, gently flipping to avoid splashing the oil. Transfer the cooked fry bread to a paper towel–lined plate, and repeat with the remaining disks.

5. In a large pan over medium heat, cook the ground beef, onion, and garlic for about 3 or 4 minutes. Add the Italian seasoning, chili powder, smoked paprika, cumin, salt, and pepper, and stir to combine. When the beef is browned, remove from the heat.

6. To assemble, add some beef and your choice of toppings to each piece of fry bread, and serve. Enjoy!

Daddy's Dirty Nachos

SERVES 4-6 | PREP TIME: 5 MINUTES | TOTAL TIME: 25 MINUTES

First off, I want to apologize to everyone and my father for calling him "Daddy." My father has never been the best cook—but he is one of my most valuable test testers! His specialty is in building and carpentry while also somehow managing all my grilling needs, thanks to working at my grandpa's little butcher shop in Wisconsin. My dad invented these walking tacos-adjacent nachos when he was making lunch for us and we ran out of regular tortilla chips.

There's a funny story behind the name of this recipe: While making these nachos during a live cooking demonstration, I was telling the story about how my dad originated the recipe. At the end of the demonstration, I accidentally dropped the entire sheet pan of nachos on the ground. Because said ground nachos were now extra dirty, the people who witnessed "Nachogate" decided we needed to call them "Daddy's Dirty Nachos." The name stuck.

1× 9-ounce (255g) package chorizo (any kind)

1× 9-ounce (255g) bag of flavored tortilla or corn chip of choice (I recommend a Doritos situation)

½ cup refried beans

1× 10-ounce (285g) block your choice cheese, grated (I like to use a sharp cheddar, fontina, or queso fresco)

1 green bell pepper, roughly chopped

½ bunch fresh cilantro, chopped

1 pint (10 ounces/285g) cherry tomatoes, quartered

1 cup iceberg lettuce, shredded

Pickled red onions, homemade or store-bought (optional)

Extra hot sauce, for serving

For the sauce

1 cup sour cream

1 tablespoon chipotle peppers in adobo sauce (or less if you don't like heat)

Zest and juice of ½ lime

1. Preheat the oven to 350°F (180°C).

2. In a medium saucepan over medium heat, brown the chorizo for 6 to 8 minutes. Remove from the heat and set aside.

3. Spread the tortilla chips on a rimmed baking sheet and then evenly distribute the refried beans, cheese, and chorizo over the top. (Be sure the cheese is spread out evenly to avoid it flattening or bubbling too much.) Bake for 10 to 15 minutes, checking occasionally—we dont want it to get too crispy.

4. Meanwhile, make the sauce. In a small bowl, combine the sour cream, chipotle peppers, and lime zest and juice.

5. Remove the nachos from the oven when the cheese is melty. Garnish with green peppers, cilantro, cherry tomatoes, iceberg lettuce, pickled red onions, if using, and hot sauce, and serve. Enjoy!

········· **TIP** ·············

You can make these nachos in the microwave when you're in a hurry. Omit the chorizo, or substitute any leftover cooked ground meat, and assemble the chips, beans, cheese, and cooked meat on a plate. Cook on high for 3 minutes or until the cheese is melty, garnish as directed, and serve, personally I like to watch it like a hawk, for the perfect melty cheese .

Ingredients

1½ cups all-purpose flour

2 teaspoons sugar

Pinch of salt

2 teaspoons baking powder

¾ cup milk of choice

1 large egg

2 hot dogs or brats (your preferred variety), cut in half so you have 4× 3-inch (7.5cm) pieces total

1× 8-ounce (225g) block cheese of choice, cut into pieces about the same size as the hot dogs, about 1×3 inches (2.5×7.5cm)

2 cups vegetable oil, for frying

Serve with

Hot dog dipping sauce and fried potato situation of choice

Special equipment

Wooden skewers

Tall, skinny glass the corndog will fit in

Thermometer

Korean-Inspired Corn Dogs

SERVES 6-8 | PREP TIME: 15 MINUTES | TOTAL TIME: 45 MINUTES

One perhaps unfortunate thing about living in a place where you don't have immediate access to all the viral foods you see on social media is that you have to make them yourself. This is one of those foods. When Korean corn dogs took control of the internet, I knew I wanted to eat them and had to figure out how to make them myself because the nearest place that sells a product like this is more than five hours away. That being said, these are incredible, and I'm glad I have the knowledge to make them at home. Now you can, too!

1. In a large bowl, combine the all-purpose flour, sugar, salt, baking powder, milk, and egg until it's the consistency of fluffy pancake batter. Pop the batter in the fridge while you prepare the skewers.

2. Begin by adding the hot dog pieces to the skewers first, followed by the cheese chunks. Leave about 3 inches (7.5cm) of the wooden skewers exposed so you can handle them while frying. Set aside.

3. Using a rubber spatula or spoon, fill a tall glass with the batter, leaving a little bit of room near the top of the cup to prevent overflows.

4. In a deep pot or Dutch oven over medium-high heat, heat the oil to 350°F (180°C).

5. Dip each first skewer into the batter-filled cup until the hot dogs and cheese pieces are fully covered, remove it from the cup, and carefully pop it into the oil. Fry the skewers in batches for about 4 or 5 minutes per side and then flip them over and fry for 4 or 5 more minutes. (The skewers will float for the most part. Frying in batches keeps the oil temperature from dropping too low.) Transfer the cooked skewers to a paper towel–lined plate to drain, and repeat with the remaining skewers.

6. Serve the corn dogs immediately with your favorite hot dog dipping sauce and fried potato situation for the best cheese pulls. Enjoy!

Juicy Lucy Meatball Sliders

SERVES 4–6 (MAKES 4, 6, OR 8 SANDWICHES, DEPENDING ON YOUR BREAD)
PREP TIME: 10 MINUTES | TOTAL TIME: 35 MINUTES

Everyone knows what a meatball is, but do you know what a juicy Lucy is? One of the pride and joys of the Upper Midwest, specifically Minnesota, it's a ground beef patty filled with melty cheese and served in burger form. It's worth living for! I decided to make it a little Italian and cuter with these sliders. It's my spin on a classic meatball sandwich with a touch of the Midwest. You'll love it!

1. In a medium bowl, mix together the ground pork, onion powder, garlic powder, smoked paprika, Italian seasoning, cayenne pepper, if using, panko breadcrumbs, ¼ cup Parmesan, sun-dried tomatoes, and the egg until sticky and well combined.

2. Using an ice cream scoop, scoop the meat into uniform balls. Press your thumb into the ball, fill the hole with 1 or 2 balls of mozzarella, and then squeeze the meat back over the hole and roll into a ball. Repeat with the remaining meat. You should have about 24–28 meatballs.

3. In a medium skillet or nonstick pan over medium heat, heat the sun-dried tomato oil. Add the meatballs, and cook on all sides for about 2 minutes per side or until you get a brown crusty edge all around. When the meatballs are cooked, add the marinara sauce to heat up and add additional flavor. (It's okay if some cheese comes out of the meatballs; it will crisp up!)

4. Preheat the oven to 350°F (180°C) or preheat the broiler.

5. In a small bowl, combine the softened butter and garlic.

6. Add the brioche buns to a nonstick baking sheet. Butter one half of the buns with the garlic butter and then add 3–4 meatballs each with some sauce. To the other side of the bun, add a slice of provolone and top with some parsley and load it up with Parmesan like they do at Olive Garden on each sandwich. Bake for 15 minutes, or broil for 5, or until the cheese is nice and melty!

7. When the sandwich is finished cooking, remove from the oven. Place the provolone, parsley, and Parmesan side of the bun over the other side to make a sandwich, and serve. Enjoy!

1 pound (450g) ground pork or ground protein of choice

2 teaspoons onion powder

1 teaspoon garlic powder

1 teaspoon smoked paprika

½ tablespoon Italian seasoning

1 teaspoon cayenne pepper (optional)

¼ cup panko breadcrumbs

¼ cup grated Parmesan, divided

3 tablespoons sun-dried tomatoes, finely chopped, oil reserved

1 large egg

8 ounces (225g) small mozzarella balls (ciliegine)

1-2 tablespoons sun-dried tomato oil, for frying

1½-2 cups marinara sauce

4 tablespoons unsalted butter, softened

4-6 garlic cloves, minced

10 brioche bread buns, sliced lengthwise across the top, like a hot dog bun

4 slices provolone, cut in half

¼ cup chopped fresh parsley, divided

6 tablespoons unsalted butter, divided

3 white or yellow onions, sliced

2 tablespoons sherry

Dash of salt

Dash of freshly ground black pepper

2–3 tablespoons light brown sugar, divided

1 baguette or French loaf, cut horizontally

1× 8-ounce (225g) wheel Brie, sliced into strips and rind removed

6 ounces (170g) prosciutto

Handful of arugula

2–3 sprigs of thyme (optional)

Balsamic glaze or fig jam

Dance-Worthy Caramelized Onion and Brie Melts

SERVES 1-2 | PREP TIME: 30 MINUTES | TOTAL TIME: 1 HOUR

On the day I created this dish, I was craving French onion soup but I was out of broth. So I had to improvise, and I'm so glad I did! The name speaks for itself. I am not going to lie to you: this recipe does take a little bit longer to prepare than the typical sandwich, but it's a treat-yourself kind of sandwich that you make when you WANT to spend a little time in the kitchen. I originally wanted to make a song to go along with this dish based on Juicy J's "Bandz a Make Her Dance" called "Sands a Make Me Dance." It's dumb, but I seriously considered it.

1. In a large pan over medium heat, melt 3 tablespoons butter. Add the onions, and sauté, stirring occasionally, for about 15 minutes.

2. Add the remaining 3 tablespoons butter, sherry, salt, pepper, and 2 tablespoons brown sugar, and cook, stirring occasionally, for 30 minutes. You should end up with a dark brown, jammy sauce. Remove from the heat, and set aside to cool for about 5 minutes.

3. Preheat the broiler.

4. Add the baguette to a baking sheet. Place slices of Brie on one side of the bread, and add prosciutto on the other side. Top the prosciutto with the remaining brown sugar, and broil for 3 to 5 minutes or until the prosciutto is crispy and the cheese is melty.

5. Remove from the oven. Add the caramelized onions, arugula, fresh thyme, if using, and a layer of balsamic glaze to the prosciutto side. Place the Brie side of the bread over the other side to make a sandwich, slice in half, and serve. Enjoy!

2

CRAVINGS FOR OCCASIONS & IRL (IN REAL LIFE)

INCLUSIVITY

You can be inclusive with food; it just takes time. I want everyone to be able to share what they love, and I try to keep things inclusive because I don't want anyone to feel left out. I want you to feel SEEN. As someone who was very shy growing up—an introvert who feigns being an extrovert—I am not very good at asking for what I want. Although I grew up in a loving family, I still experienced loneliness from time to time, and I still do as an adult.

When you reach the age at which you notice that you're different from other kids but you're not entirely sure why that is, it can be kind of stressful. As a kid, I wanted to be a pop diva or a painter, but I didn't really have a lot of role models. I think it's important to see other people like you in your environment. I didn't really see a lot of other people like me until I was around age twelve, when we all went from playing outside to sending messages on MSN Messenger and then being online. I'm so happy to see a new generation of people being so strong and sure of themselves. I find it really beautiful and inspiring. Their confidence speaks volumes and gives me hope for the future.

I selected a lot of the recipes in this part because I wanted to include some of my favorite foods from various cultures, like my parents modeled for me growing up. Food, like people, comes in all shapes, sizes, and flavors. I know trying new things can be scary, but hopefully, this book will inspire you to try new foods, which can then become some of your new favorites.

THE MEAT & POTATOES OF THINGS

Pierogies, 2 Ways

SERVES 4–6 (ABOUT 25–30 PIEROGI, OR 5–6 PER PERSON; I RECOMMEND
DOUBLING THE RECIPE BECAUSE EVERYONE WILL COME BACK FOR SECONDS)
PREP TIME: 10 MINUTES | TOTAL TIME: 1 HOUR (PLUS 30 MINUTES RESTING TIME)

**Remember when I was talking about how my Great–Grandma Lucille
came to live with us? She brought a new dynamic to the household
when she moved in. She introduced us to interesting foods, helped
around the house, and told entertaining (and sometimes sad) stories
about the Great Depression. We learned a lot. This is one of her dishes
that made it onto our regular meal rotation. I think of her every time I
make it.**

**Potatoes are quite literally one of my favorite things, and if you were to
ask me my favorite food, I would tell you french fries. The best way to
describe pierogi to someone who's never had one? Think of them like
little potato dumplings or ravioli, filled with even more potato! Anyone
who tries them falls in love with them. By making them from scratch,
you'll know what a labor of love making them can be. Disclaimer: it's
totally worth it.**

1. In a large pot of salted water over medium-high heat, cook the russet
potatoes for 15 to 20 minutes or until they're fork-tender.

2. Meanwhile, in a medium pan over medium-low heat, heat the olive oil. Add
the onion and garlic, and sauté for 4 to 6 minutes or until soft and translucent.

3. Drain the potatoes. Transfer the half to a large bowl and leave the remaining
half in the pot.

4. To the potatoes in the pot, add the cooked onion, garlic, salt, pepper, cream
cheese, and cheddar, mashing with a potato masher or ricer as you go until well
combined and the potatoes are silky and soft, about 5 to 10 minutes.

5. Mash the bowl of warm potatoes using a potato masher until minimal lumps
remain. Add the butter, all-purpose flour, salt, the sour cream, egg, and warm
water. Using a rubber spatula or fork, mix for about 5 to 8 minutes or until the
dough is smooth and slightly sticky.

6. Turn out the dough onto a lightly floured surface, and knead with your hands
for 3 to 5 minutes. Let the dough rest, covered, for 30 minutes on the counter.

7. If using a pasta roller, divide the dough in half and use the machine to roll it
out 2 sheets of pasta, about 3 x 11-inch (7½ x 28cm) each). If rolling by hand,
divide the dough in half, and use a rolling pin coated with flour, if needed, to roll
out the dough into two 3 x 11-inch (7½ x 28cm) strips.

2½–3 pounds (1.25–1.5kg) russet or
   Yukon Gold potatoes, peeled and cut
   into 1-inch (2.5cm) cubes (about 3–4
   potatoes)

6 tablespoons unsalted butter, for
   pan-frying

Sautéed onion, tomato sauce, grated
   Parmesan, crumbled bacon, crumbled
   bleu cheese, and chopped scallions,
   for garnish (optional; mix and match
   to your heart's content!)

For the dough

2 tablespoons unsalted butter

2½–3 cups all-purpose flour, plus
   extra for dusting

Dash of salt

¼ cup sour cream, plus extra
   for garnish

1 egg

⅔ cup warm water

For the filling

2 tablespoons extra virgin olive oil

1 white or yellow onion, finely chopped

4 garlic cloves, minced

Salt and freshly ground black pepper

4 ounces (115g) cream cheese (about
   ½× 8-ounce/225g block)

1 cup shredded cheddar

Special equipment

Rolling pin

Potato masher or ricer

Pasta roller (optional)

Pierogi maker or ravioli press (optional)

> ·········· **TIP** ··········
>
> If you're feeling a little
> extra, fry the pierogies
> in bacon fat!

8. To assemble using a pierogi maker or ravioli press, add 1- or 2-tablespoon dollops of the potato mixture to one of the strips of dough. You should be able to get roughly 25 to 30 evenly spaced dollops. Add the other strip on top, and section into individual perogies, like ravioli, or seal the edges using the pierogi tool or a fork to press the edges, doing your best to keep the filling tucked in.

9. Bring a large pot with 6 cups of water to a boil over medium-high heat. Working in batches, add the pierogi to the boiling water and gently stir so they don't stick to each other. Cook for 5 to 6 minutes per batch or until they float. Transfer to a plate, and repeat with the remaining pierogies.

10. You can either serve the boiled pierogies as is with your desired garnishes, or pan-fry them first. I prefer to pan-fry! To do this: add the butter to the pan used to sautée the onion and garlic, and melt over medium-high heat. Working in batches, fry the boiled pierogi for about 2 minutes per side, adding more butter as needed, or until slightly brown and crispy. Transfer to a plate, and repeat with the remaining pierogi.

11. Garnish with your favorite garnishes, and serve.

Summer Beer Butt Chicken

SERVES 6-8 | PREP TIME: 10 MINUTES | TOTAL TIME: 1 HOUR 30 MINUTES

This recipe is so reminiscent of my summers in Wisconsin because we used to make this dish over the campfire at my grandma's house. We loved making beer butt chicken because of the notion of inserting the beer can into the chicken's cavity, which was hilarious as a kid. But gosh dangit, that chicken comes out so tender and juicy. Man, oh, man. If this isn't one of the best chicken dishes you've had over a campfire (or from your oven), then I'll can it and shut up.

1. Lower the oven rack if necessary to accommodate an upright chicken. Preheat the oven to 450°F (230°C).

2. In a small bowl, whisk together the remaining summer shandy, brown sugar, lemon juice, onion powder, lemon pepper seasoning, crushed red pepper flakes, 1 tablespoon salt, 1 tablespoon pepper, garlic powder, and olive oil. Be sure your chicken has been patted dry and use the two- or three-finger method to rub the mixture all over the chicken, front and back.

3. Stuff the chicken with garlic, rosemary, and the juiced lemon halves. Place the celery, carrots, and onions on the bottom of a large casserole dish or roasting pan, make a well for the beer can to hold the chicken. Place the open beer can into the well and then carefully place the chicken on top of the can, so it's standing upright with the can inside the cavity.

4. Place the dish in the oven, keeping the chicken upright, and bake for 10 minutes. Reduce the heat to 350°F (180°C), and cook for 1 hour. During the last 10 minutes, pull the bird out of the oven and cover it with butter. Using tongs, turn the chicken, with the beer can still inserted, and bake for 10 minutes more.

5. Remove the can from the chicken, slice the chicken as desired, and serve with the roasted veggies. Enjoy! Happy end of summer!

1×12-ounce (350ml) can summer shandy or Budweiser (drink ¼ or ½ of it if you're wild, but save the can)

3–4 tablespoons brown sugar

Juice of 1 lemon (save the juiced halves for stuffing the chicken)

2 tablespoons onion powder

2 teaspoons lemon pepper seasoning

1 teaspoon crushed red pepper flakes

1 tablespoon salt

1 tablespoon freshly ground black pepper

2 tablespoons garlic powder

Healthy drizzle of olive oil (about 3 tablespoons)

1× 3½-pound (1.75kg) chicken, cleaned and patted dry

2 tablespoons fresh or dried rosemary

1 head of garlic, top removed

2 celery stalks, roughly chopped

2 carrots, roughly chopped

2 white or yellow onions, roughly chopped

3–4 tablespoons unsalted butter, melted

Special equipment

Beer can

· · · · · · · · · · · · · · · · TIPS · · · · · · · · · · · · · · · ·

Brining the chicken overnight in a salt and pepper brine (or any other seasonings you want to put on the chicken) makes it 10 times better, but if you don't have the time, this quick method works well, too.

If you lay down the chicken in the oven, only the top will get roasted. But if you stand it up, all sides of the cock will cook evenly! It's also important to rotate—think of this as an unusual rotisserie chicken, only we're the ones who have to do the rotating!

Make sure to arrange your oven racks ahead of time.

Chicken Tikka Masala

SERVES 2-4 | PREP TIME: 30 MINUTES | TOTAL TIME: 30 MINUTES

10 garlic cloves, minced, divided

1 tablespoon ground cumin, divided

1 tablespoon ground ginger, divided

2 teaspoons chili powder, divided

2 teaspoons ground turmeric, divided

2 teaspoons garam masala, divided

1½ cups Greek yogurt (any fat percent will work, but I use full fat)

1-2 pounds (450g-1kg) boneless, skinless chicken thighs, cut into roughly 1-inch (2.5cm) cubes

4 tablespoons olive oil, divided

2 tablespoons unsalted butter or ghee

1 yellow onion, chopped

6 ounces (170g) tomato paste

1½-2 cups low-sodium chicken broth

¼ cup heavy cream or coconut cream

1 bunch fresh cilantro or parsley, chopped, for garnish

Serve with

Cooked rice and/or naan

I didn't grow up living near a large variety of restaurants that revolved around foods other than burgers, so we always had to make non-burger food at home. I can remember the first time I had authentic Indian food. I was in college, and of course I was with one of my besties, Jessica. We love trying new restaurants and asking the staff about their favorite dishes on the menu because we're adventurous eaters with an ambition to find new flavors and experiences.

Some of our favorite spots are local, "hole in the wall" establishments that no one else knows about, so when we found an amazing little Indian restaurant in Fargo called India Palace, we had to go. We told our server (whose family owned the restaurant) we'd never had Indian food before, and they gave us the five-star treatment and fed us all the most amazing dishes and flavors. We were obsessed. It was so good, I created a Yelp! account just to leave them a review—so you KNOW it was good. No way am I claiming this to be authentic, but just one of my best attempts at making it at home.

1. In a medium bowl, combine half of the garlic, half of the spices (cumin, ginger, chili powder, turmeric, and garam masala), and all of the Greek yogurt and chicken. Cover with plastic wrap, and set aside for 30 minutes.

2. In a large pan or skillet over medium heat, add half of the olive oil and the butter. Add the chicken to the pan, and cook, stirring occasionally, for about 6 to 8 minutes or until it has a nice golden crust. Transfer the chicken to a plate.

3. Add the remaining oil, the yellow onion, and the remaining garlic to the pan, and cook for 4 to 6 minutes or until the onion and garlic start to brown. Add the tomato paste and the remaining spices, and stir.

4. Slowly pour in the chicken broth, stirring and scraping the bottom of the pan so nothing sticks.

5. Stir in the heavy cream and then return the chicken to the pan. Bring to a simmer, and cook for about 10 minutes or until smooth. Serve over warm rice or with naan, and garnish with cilantro. Enjoy!

Buttermilk Fried Chicken with Fried Potato Salad

FRIED CHICKEN SERVES 4–6 | PREP TIME: 1 HOUR (PLUS MARINATING TIME)
TOTAL TIME: 1 HOUR 30 MINUTES

POTATO SALAD SERVES 4–6 AS A SIDE DISH | PREP TIME: 5 MINUTES
TOTAL TIME: 30 MINUTES

For the picnic of your dreams, I recommend frying some of this outstanding chicken. This recipe is inspired by all the times I've gone over to eat chicken at my best friend's parents' house. When Mary Fontes, my best friend's mom and my second mother, invites you over to eat, you hustle over and get your ass in a seat. Everything that comes out of Mary's kitchen is made with love, and if you love fried chicken, even better. I thought this would pair so lovely with something else I'm passionate about—potato salad! Oh, and we're frying that, too. It's even more to love and more to share!

Buttermilk Fried Chicken

1. In a large food-safe container with a lid, whisk together the buttermilk, cayenne pepper, if using, salt, rosemary, thyme, black pepper, and garlic. Add the chicken to the brine, cover, and set in the refrigerator for at least 1 hour (or up to 12 hours).

2. Meanwhile, in a large bowl, whisk together the flour, cornstarch, baking powder, salt, smoked paprika, garlic powder, onion powder, poultry seasoning, oregano, and cayenne pepper, if using. If you want extra crunchy bits on your fried chicken, you can add 3 or 4 tablespoons of the brine to the dredge before mixing.

3. Remove the chicken from the fridge. Using tongs, remove the pieces from the brine, add to the dredge mixture, and turn to coat. When the chicken is coated, transfer to a clean plate and allow to come to room temperature until ready to fry.

4. In a Dutch oven or another heavy-bottomed pot over medium to high heat, heat the oil to 350°F (180°C).

5. Working in small batches, add the chicken to the oil, wings and legs first because they're smaller and cook faster, and cook for about 10 to 12 minutes (or 8 minutes if you have a smaller bird) or until golden brown. The internal temperature of the chicken should be 165°F (75°C).

6. Using tongs, remove the chicken from the oil, letting any excess drip off. Transfer to a baking sheet lined with a baking rack so it can stay crispy while it rests, and finish with a sprinkle of salt and black pepper. Continue frying the remaining chicken in small batches. Serve immediately, alongside Fried Potato Salad. Enjoy!

1× 3½-pound (1.75kg) chicken, cleaned and patted dry, broken down into pieces (2 breasts, 2 thighs, 2 legs, and 2 wings)

Vegetable or canola oil for frying (enough to submerge the chicken)

For the brine
3 cups buttermilk
1 teaspoon cayenne pepper (optional)
1 tablespoon salt
4 sprigs of rosemary
6 sprigs of thyme
1 teaspoon freshly ground black pepper
6 garlic cloves, crushed

For the dredge
2½ cups all-purpose flour
½ cup cornstarch
1 teaspoon baking powder
½ tablespoon salt
1 tablespoon smoked paprika
1 tablespoon garlic powder
1 tablespoon onion powder
1 tablespoon poultry seasoning
1 teaspoon dried oregano
1 teaspoon cayenne pepper (optional)

Serve with
Fried Potato Salad (recipe to follow)

Special equipment
Frying thermometer
Meat thermometer

> ·········· **TIP** ··········
>
> Try not to keep the chicken marinating for longer than 12 hours; otherwise, it can get a little too salty.

Fried Potato Salad

1. In a large pan over medium-high heat, heat the olive oil. Add the potatoes, and a generous sprinkle of salt and pepper, and fry for about 5 to 8 minutes or until the potatoes start to brown and get crisp. Transfer the potatoes to a paper towel–lined plate to drain, and sprinkle with a little more salt and pepper. Taste a little tater to be sure it's good.

2. In a large bowl, combine the mayonnaise, stone-ground mustard, red wine vinegar, hard-boiled eggs, if using, half of the dill, the red onion, and garlic powder.

3. Add the potatoes and stir to combine.

4. Place in the refrigerator to cool until ready to serve. Garnish with the remaining dill and chives, and serve. Enjoy!

¼ cup olive or peanut oil

8 cups roughly chopped russet potatoes or frozen cubed hash browns

Salt and freshly ground black pepper

1½ cups mayonnaise

1 tablespoon stone-ground mustard

1 teaspoon red wine vinegar

4 hard-boiled eggs, peeled and roughly chopped (optional)

2 tablespoons chopped fresh dill, plus extra for garnish

1 red or white onion, roughly chopped

2 teaspoons garlic powder

Handful of chopped fresh chives, for garnish

Hot Honey Chicken & Potatoes

SERVES 2-4 | PREP TIME: 10 MINUTES | TOTAL TIME: 45 MINUTES

I love hot and spicy foods, so when I first discovered hot honey, it's safe to say I couldn't get enough of it. Hot honey can be used on pizza, biscuits, goat cheese, ice cream, salads, or roasted chicken and potatoes—if you couldn't already tell from the recipe title. This dish makes me think of my favorite song by Robyn, "Honey." The sweet heat is as addictive as the song. So come get your honey, baby!

1. Bring a large pot half full of water to a boil over medium-high heat. Drop in the yellow potatoes, and boil for 5 to 10 minutes or until the potatoes are fork-tender. Drain and set aside.

2. Preheat the oven to 450°F (230°C).

3. In a large bowl, coat the chicken with the onion powder, garlic powder, sage, Italian seasoning, smoked paprika, salt, pepper and 3 tablespoons of olive oil.

4. In a large cast-iron or oven-safe skillet over medium-high heat, heat about 1 tablespoon of olive oil. Add the potatoes and ½ of the shallot, and cook for 5 to 10 minutes. When the vegetables start to turn brown, push them to the side, add a little more oil, and then add the chicken. Cook the chicken for 5 minutes per side or until it has a golden crust.

5. When the crust has formed, place the chicken on top of the potatoes so there's room to make the sauce in the skillet. Add the rest of the shallot, butter, hot sauce, chicken broth, crushed red pepper flakes, and honey, and bring to a simmer. When the honey bubbles, toss the chicken and potatoes in the sauce to coat and then transfer the skillet to the oven.

6. Bake for 30 minutes or until the chicken's internal temperature reaches 165°F (75°C). Remove from the oven. Spoon more sauce over the chicken and potatoes, garnish with crushed red pepper flakes and chives, if using, and serve. Enjoy!

1½ pounds (680g) yellow potatoes, quartered

4 chicken thighs (about 1½–2 pounds/680g–1kg)

½ tablespoon onion powder

½ tablespoon garlic powder

1 teaspoon dried sage

½ tablespoon Italian seasoning

1 teaspoon smoked paprika

3 tablespoons extra virgin olive oil, plus more for frying

1 shallot, minced and divided

Salt and freshly ground black pepper

3 tablespoons unsalted butter

¼ cup or more of hot sauce of choice (I use Franks RedHot)

¼ cup chicken broth

1-2 tablespoons crushed red pepper flakes, plus extra for garnish (optional)

5 tablespoons honey

Handful of finely chopped fresh chives or parsley, for garnish (optional)

Special equipment

Meat thermometer

Campfire Meals

SERVES 4-6 (PEOPLE, NOT BEARS) | PREP TIME: 10 MINUTES
TOTAL TIME: 25-30 MINUTES

1 pound (450g) ground beef or pork
(any fat percentage)

1 white or yellow onion, roughly
chopped

12 ounces (340g) frozen vegetables of
choice

4-5 garlic cloves, minced

16 ounces (450g) frozen hash browns

1 bell pepper (any color), ribs and seeds
removed and roughly chopped

1 tablespoon Lawry's Seasoned Salt, or
salt and freshly ground black pepper

1 tablespoon sweet paprika

1 tablespoon Italian seasoning

1 cup shredded low-moisture
mozzarella or cheddar, divided

5-6 tablespoons unsalted butter, cut
into 1-tablespoon chunks

Serve with

Ketchup or Homemade Ranch Dressing
(see page 212)

Fresh herbs, like parsley, rosemary,
basil, chives (whatever you have)

Special equipment

Campfire

Griddle

Meat thermometer (optional)

We've made all types of campfire meals (or campfire hot dishes) over the firepit at my grandma's cabin, from hand pies, to fish, to any brat or hot dog situation, to soups, to s'mores—the whole nine yards. These times are some of the happiest memories of my life. As a bonus: I also learned fire safety.

Our main concern, or worry, at Grandma's cabin was and still is bears. (No, not the cute, fuzzy ones, like me.) We usually get at least one furry visitor every other week during the summer. They love my grandma's leftovers, and I totally get it. My grandma is a dope cook. I'd eat out of her garbage too, if I was that kind of bear.

This dish can best be described as a "deconstructed hot dish." And remember, only you can prevent forest fires!

1. Be sure the campfire is stoked, or prepare some hot coals for the griddle over a medium-high-heat fire, either directly over the fire or 65 to 70 percent over the main flame or hot coals.

2. Cover your work surface with a large sheet of foil. Layer all the ingredients on top of the foil, starting with the ground beef, onion, vegetables, garlic, hash browns, bell pepper, seasonings, and a layer of mozzarella. Put the butter chunks in a line on top, so they can evenly distribute as they melt.

3. Fold the edges of the foil inward to create a package, and roll the seams down to create a seal. Use another sheet of foil to cover, if needed.

4. Add the foil packet on top of the fire, and cook for about 15 to 20 minutes or until the beef reaches at least 160°F (70°C). About halfway through the cook time, pull the packet to the side and pop it open. I like to give it a light stir to be sure the meat is cooking. If it's not, put it over a hotter section of the fire. Let it cool a bit before serving.

5. Garnish with the remaining mozzarella or fresh herbs, or serve with ketchup, Homemade Ranch Dressing, your favorite dipping sauces. Enjoy!

······· TIPS ·······

If making this over a fire pit, you'll need a
good medium-sized fire. Use a grill pan or
something sturdy to support the foil. This
works incredibly well if you have a firepit
with a shelf and arm attachment.

If making this in an oven, you can throw all
the ingredients into a casserole dish, cover it
with foil or a lid, and bake at 350°F (180°C)
for 20 to 30 minutes, checking for doneness
halfway through the cooking time.

If you want to make this for breakfast,
replace the beef with 1 pound breakfast
sausage or bacon.

It's okay to use one or two layers of foil, but
try to use some reusable cast-iron instead!

Chicken Marsala

SERVES 3-4 | PREP TIME: 10 MINUTES | TOTAL TIME: 25 MINUTES

Not to be confused with an Indian tikka masala, but more inspired by Italian American cooking, this dish is composed of tender, golden, pan-fried chicken, mushrooms, and Marsala wine. When my friend Jessica and I were in college, we worked at an Italian restaurant, and this was her favorite dish. So I had to learn how to recreate it for her (and for me). Easy, breezy, creamy, Chicken Marsala!

1. Place the chicken on a sheet of plastic wrap, and top the chicken with a second layer so things don't get too messy. Using a meat pounder (or a rolling pin if you don't have one), pound the chicken to about ½- to ¼-inch (1.25cm–6mm) thick. Remove the plastic wrap and liberally season both sides of the chicken with salt and pepper.

2. To make the dredge, in a large bowl, combine the flour, onion powder, and more salt and pepper. Add the chicken, and turn to coat on all sides. Transfer the chicken to a plate.

3. In a large, oven-safe pan or skillet over medium heat, add 1 tablespoon olive oil, the butter, and the thyme. Add the chicken, and cook for about 8 minutes per side or until the outside has turned golden and the internal temp reaches 165°F (75°C).

4. Transfer the chicken to a clean plate. Add the remaining 1 tablespoon of olive oil to the pan if needed. Add the onion, baby bella mushrooms, and garlic, and sauté for 4 to 6 minutes or until browned. Add the Marsala wine, and bring to a simmer to cook out any alcohol, about 10 minutes tops. Stir in the heavy cream.

5. You can either return the chicken to the pan and coat in the sauce or drizzle on as much sauce as you'd like to the chicken on the plate. Garnish with parsley, and serve with pasta, a salad, or a starch. Enjoy!

2½ pounds (1.25kg) boneless, skinless chicken breasts

Salt and freshly ground black pepper

½ cup all-purpose flour

1 teaspoon onion powder

2 tablespoons olive oil, divided

3 tablespoons unsalted butter

4 sprigs of thyme

1 white or yellow onion, sliced

6 ounces (170g) baby bella mushrooms, sliced

4–6 garlic cloves, minced or pressed

½ cup dry or sweet Marsala wine (I prefer sweet)

¼ cup heavy cream

½ bunch fresh parsley, chopped, for garnish

Serve with
Pasta, a salad, or a starchy situation

Special equipment
Meat pounder or rolling pin

Meat thermometer

Ingredients

¼ cup olive oil

4–6 thinly sliced chicken breasts (about 20–31 ounces/560–880g)

Salt and freshly ground black pepper

2 teaspoon onion powder

1 teaspoon crushed red pepper flakes

1 teaspoon fresh or dried oregano

1 teaspoon fresh or dried basil

1½ teaspoons anchovy paste, or 3–4 anchovies, minced

1 teaspoon grated garlic or 2–3 cloves, minced (but paste is best for this)

1 teaspoon Dijon mustard

1 egg

3 tablespoons freshly grated Parmesan, or to taste, plus more for serving

2–3 heads of romaine lettuce, halved or quartered

Special equipment

Meat thermometer

Pan-Seared Chicken Caesar

SERVES 4-6 | PREP TIME: 10 MINUTES | TOTAL TIME: 25 MINUTES

It wouldn't be a cookbook without some sort of chicken Caesar salad situation, right? I originally wanted to include my take on a classic C-sal, but that seemed too boring. I decided to make it into a quick weeknight dinner instead. I love sneaking vegetables and greens into my body in the form of lettuce boats for crunchy elements.

1. Season the chicken with a heavy pinch of salt and pepper. To a pan over medium heat, heat the olive oil. When the oil is shimmering, add the chicken, half of the onion powder, red pepper flakes, oregano, and basil. Cook for 5 to 7 minutes. Flip over the chicken and season with more salt and pepper. Cook for 5 to 7 minutes more or until the internal temperature is at least 165°F (75°C). Transfer the chicken to a plate. Let the oil in the pan cool down for a hot minute.

2. To the warm oil, add the anchovy paste, garlic, and Dijon mustard, and whisk to combine.

3. Add the egg and Parmesan, and whisk until the dressing is smooth and creamy. It's probably going to be a little salty, so taste and adjust the salt if necessary and then add a couple turns of freshly cracked pepper.

4. Return the chicken to the pan and coat in the sauce.

5. Divide the romaine among the serving plates, add a chicken breast per plate and some dressing on top, and serve. Enjoy!

TIPS

You can serve this with mashed potatoes and some green beans if you like, or get crazy and throw it in a wrap with some greens!

The oil is going to cook the egg which is going to make everything SO creamy, trust the process!

Weeknight Salmon & Dilly Potatoes

SERVES 3-4 | PREP TIME: 5 MINUTES | TOTAL TIME: 45 MINUTES

I don't know about you, but I used to be so intimidated by cooking fish. I think my biggest issue was that I didn't really care for the leftover skin. Or maybe it was having to take something out of the freezer and wait for it to thaw and hope I still would be in the mood to prepare the fish when it was ready. I've since gotten over that bad attitude by reaching out and asking my friends for fish recipes that I could experiment with when I started doing more meal-prepping. I quickly learned that cooking fish is genuinely so easy! Anyone can do this!

You know how when you're having a depressive episode (or maybe that's just me) and you're not being very nice to yourself, saying, you need an effortlessly easy but nutritious meal—enough to keep the train a-chuggin' if you know what I mean? This might be the answer! What I do when I'm not feeling so swell in my brain is to make dinner with a friend, in person or over the phone. It really helps!

16 ounces (450g) fingerling potatoes

8 garlic cloves, minced, divided

2 lemons, 1 to be juiced and the other sliced, for garnish

3 tablespoons stone-ground mustard

2 tablespoons sambal oelek

2½ tablespoons hot honey

1 teaspoon smoked paprika

1 teaspoon Italian seasoning

1 tablespoon extra-virgin olive oil, plus more for frying

Salt and freshly ground black pepper

½ tablespoon dried dill

3-4 salmon fillets (about 21-28 ounces/600-800g total)

Serve with

Sour cream, flaky salt, chopped fresh dill, and malt or white vinegar for drizzling

> ········· **TIP** ·········
>
> You can skip the taters and instead add some vegetables or a salad and starchy things. Or turn the crispy potatoes into quick mashed potatoes.

1. Preheat the oven to 350°F (180°C).

2. Bring a large pot with 5 or 6 cups of water to a boil over medium-high heat. Add the fingerling potatoes, and boil for about 15 minutes or until fork-tender.

3. In a small bowl, combine half the garlic, the lemon juice, mustard, sambal oelek, hot honey, smoked paprika, and Italian seasoning.

4. Drain the potatoes and add to a large oven-safe pan or skillet and toss them with the olive oil. Using the bottom of a glass and light pressure, crush the potatoes until they're about ½ inch (1.25cm) thick. Sprinkle the remaining garlic over the potatoes along with the dill. Season generously with salt and pepper. Bake for 20 to 25 minutes. You want them to be crispy!

5. In a large pan over medium heat, heat some olive oil. Lightly coat the salmon fillets with sauce, and place in the pan. Cook for 5 minutes, flip once, and cook for 5 minutes on the other side. You want it to be flaky, and it cooks quickly!

6. Add the salmon to a plate, and cover with sauce. Add the potatoes alongside. Top with sour cream, flaky salt, the remaining lemon slices, fresh dill, or vinegar, and serve. Enjoy!

About 3 pounds (1.5kg) bone-in short ribs, at room temperature

1 tablespoon salt

3 tablespoons extra virgin olive oil

1 sweet yellow onion, roughly chopped

6 celery stalks, roughly chopped

1 leek, washed and roughly chopped

1 shallot, roughly chopped

¾ cup tomato paste

2 heads of garlic

3 dried or fresh bay leaves

½ bunch fresh rosemary

½ bunch fresh thyme

2 cups red or white wine

1 tablespoon whole black peppercorns

2 Anaheim or guajillo chile peppers

4 cups beef broth

Chopped green onion, for garnish

····· **TIPS** ·····

Let the meat come to room temperature before cooking so that it can evenly cook all the way through (kind of like a giant fancy steak).

Serve with mashed potatoes or the starchy situation of your choice.

Try making this recipe with bison or venison!

Roast with the Most

SERVES 6-8 | PREP TIME: 20 MINUTES | TOTAL TIME: 1 HOUR 20 MINUTES

For my birthday, my brother (who is also a professional cook) made this delicious roast, and it was so melt-in-your-mouth tender that I'd feel like a clod if I didn't share the recipe with you. He definitely received the "good cook" gene from my mom. This recipe has all the things you love about a "traditional" roast but with double the flavor. I always say that food tastes better when someone else is making it. It was true for this birthday roast, but I'll let you be the final judge!

1. Preheat the oven to 350°F (180°C).

2. Season the short ribs on all sides with salt.

3. In a large oven-safe pan or Dutch oven over medium-high heat, heat the oil. Add the short ribs, and sear on all sides for 9 or 10 minutes total or until they develop a nice crust on the outside. When all sides are browned, transfer to a platter and set aside.

4. Add the yellow onion, celery, leek, shallot, and tomato paste to the pan, and cook, stirring occasionally, for 8 to 10 minutes or until softened.

5. Add the garlic, bay leaves, rosemary, thyme, red wine, peppercorns, chile peppers, and beef broth to the pan, and stir.

6. Return the ribs back to the pan. They'll cook down in the sauce. Cover and roast in the oven for at least 1 hour and up to 2 hours. Check halfway through the cook time to see if you need to add more wine or broth. When the ribs are done, the meat should perfectly slide off the bone.

7. Remove from the oven, and remove and discard the bay leaves. Garnish with chopped green onions, and serve. Enjoy!

Rosemary & Garlic Butter Steak Kabobs

**SERVES 6-8 | PREP TIME: 1 HOUR (OR OVERNIGHT FOR MARINATING)
TOTAL TIME: 1 HOUR 20 MINUTES**

Minnesota summers are sacred, like a country song. It's light until nearly 10 p.m.! So we have to squeeze all the warm, breezy, dreamy, wedding-filled, romantic-campfire summer nights into the short amount of time we have. Kabobs are something we make every week in the summer, in rotation with burgers and hot dogs. Of course, I added some pesto on top for this version because pesto is great on most things. This recipe can be altered in so many ways to fit your preferences.

1. In a large bowl, whisk together the olive oil, soy sauce, red wine vinegar, mustard, lemon juice, garlic, and rosemary. Add the sirloin steaks, shrimp (if using), onions, and zucchini. Cover with plastic wrap and marinate for 1 hour or up to 24 hours in the fridge.

2. Assemble the skewers by adding the marinated steak, shrimp, a couple slices of onion, zucchini, bell peppers, tomato, and baby bella mushrooms. Discard the rest of the marinade.

3. Heat a grill or grill pan to medium-high.

4. Cook the kabobs according to how you like your protein cooked: rare, medium, or even well done. I like my steak medium rare-ish. This usually takes a total of 10 to 12 minutes, rotating every 4 minutes. A good indication is to look at the shrimp, which will cook faster than the steak.

5. Remove the kabobs from the grill, and let them rest for 3 to 5 minutes.

6. Liberally brush the kabobs with melted butter followed by a drizzle of Delishaas Pesto, if using. Garnish with parsley, and serve. Enjoy!

¼ cup olive oil

¼ cup soy sauce

1 tablespoon red wine vinegar

1 tablespoon coarse-ground mustard

Juice of 2 lemons or limes

5-6 garlic cloves, minced

3 tablespoons chopped fresh rosemary

3-4 pounds (1.5-2kg) sirloin steaks

1 pound (450g) peeled and deveined shrimp (optional)

2 red or white onions, quartered

2 zucchini, cut into 1-inch (2.5cm) slices

2-3 bell peppers (any color), ribs and seeds removed and quartered

6-8 medium tomatoes

6-8 baby bella mushrooms, cut in half and stem trimmed or removed

8 tablespoons unsalted butter, melted

Delishaas Pesto (see page 127)

Handful of chopped fresh parsley, for garnish

Special equipment

Grill or grill pan

Wooden or metal skewers

········· **TIPS** ·················

If using wooden skewers, soak them in a glass of water for a few minutes before threading on the kebab ingredients. This will prevent burnt wood in your food.

Use whatever meat works best for you, or what's affordable! For the best results, marinate everything for as long as you can—up to 24 hours for the tenderest meat!

If your kabob gets tooooo heavy, add a second skewer, especially if using wood.

As a general rule, I like to assemble a few skewers of just vegetables or just seafood if I have any vegetarian or pescatarian friends coming to dinner and cook them away from the meat kabobs. Cook the vegetable kabobs first, before the protein, to avoid cross-contamination.

OH, THE PASTA-BILITIES

Creamy Sun-dried Tomato & Lemon Pasta

SERVES 3-4 | PREP TIME: 5 MINUTES | TOTAL TIME: 30 MINUTES

This is one of my most viral recipes and the best-tasting pasta dish I've invented to date. I said what I said. I quite literally only make this once a month because when I do, I'll eat an entire pound of pasta in less than 24 hours (which means I eat it for dinner, as a midnight snack, and then again for breakfast). This is also my favorite recipe to make for a date—so you're welcome ahead of time (*wink*).

A couple of tips with this recipe: if you can't find sun-dried tomato paste, don't sweat it! I've tested this recipe with jarred sun-dried tomatoes that have been puréed and even red pesto (pesto with sun-dried tomatoes). Also, I recommend tasting as you go when it comes to the lemon and crushed red pepper flakes because you can always add more but you cannot take away. I'm a huge advocate of lemon and spice, so of course I like a lot in this dish.

1 tablespoon extra-virgin olive oil

3 large shallots, thinly sliced

2 teaspoons Italian seasoning

2 teaspoons dried basil

1 teaspoon crushed red pepper flakes, plus extra for garnish (or double for extra spice)

Zest and juice of 1 large lemon (or double for extra citrus)

1× 2.8-ounce (80g) tube sun-dried tomato paste

1 cup heavy cream

2 cups mixed greens or spinach

½ cup grated Parmesan

1 pound (450g) paccheri pasta (use a fat rigatoni if you can't find it)

Burrata and chopped fresh parsley, for garnish

1. In a large pan over medium to high heat, heat the extra virgin olive oil. Add the shallots, and cook for about 3 minutes or until translucent. Add the Italian seasoning, basil, crushed red pepper flakes, lemon zest, and lemon juice, and cook for 5 minutes.

2. Add the heavy cream, and when it starts to bubble, add the mixed greens and Parmesan. Season with salt and pepper.

3. At the same time, in another large pan, cook the pasta in boiling water according to the package directions. (I prefer al dente, but do your thing.) Drain, reserving 1 cup pasta water.

4. Add the pasta to the sauce, and toss to coat. Add the reserved pasta water, and continue to toss.

5. Tear open the ball of burrata, and use it to top the serving bowls of pasta. Garnish with parsley and extra crushed red pepper flakes, if using, and serve. Enjoy!

Dad's Favorite Shrimp Scampi with Grandma Mary's Homemade Pasta

SCAMPI SERVES 4-6 | PREP TIME: 5 MINUTES | TOTAL TIME: 30 MINUTES

PASTA YIELD 2 LB (1 KG) PASTA | PREP TIME: 20 MINUTES
TOTAL TIME: 1 HOUR (INCLUDING THE DRYING PROCESS)

This is one of my dad's favorite pasta dishes so we make it for him every Father's Day and birthday. If you are a lover of lemon, you will thoroughly enjoy this, too.

I think cooking with wine sometimes intimidates people, but it's wayyyyyy easier than you think. You can also buy cooking wine in the cooking section of your grocery store if you're not old enough or have no desire to go into a liquor store. If you're worried about wasting money on a bottle of wine, thinking you'll ruin the dish, don't be. Buy an inexpensive bottle, use that until you master the dish, and then you can move on to the good stuff. That way you can sip on some of the wine and tune into your favorite playlist while you hone your culinary skills.

This pasta has the perfect sharp twang of citrus that pairs so well with the juicy seafood and a nice salty cheese. It's crave-worthy! I'm a fan of making this for a midnight snack, but it's also perfect for hot summery days, because it's so delicious served cold or eaten right out of the refrigerator as leftovers.

For the shrimp scampi

4 tablespoons unsalted butter, divided

8 ounces (225g) large shrimp, peeled, deveined, tails removed, and patted dry, thawed if frozen

6-8 garlic cloves, minced (or more, if you're a garlic girl like me)

1 teaspoon Italian seasoning

1 teaspoon fresh or dried oregano, plus extra if fresh for garnish

1 pound (450g) linguine or homemade pasta

9 ounces (255g) canned quartered artichoke hearts, drained

2 tablespoons capers

¼ cup Kalamata olives, pitted and sliced

2 teaspoons anchovy paste

Juice of ½ lemon

½ cup white wine (I prefer pinot grigio)

1 cup spinach

Grated Parmesan, and sliced lemon, for garnish

For the homemade pasta

2 large eggs

1½ cup all-purpose flour, plus extra for dusting

Olive oil, for coating

Special equipment

Rolling pin or noodle stick

Dad's Favorite Shrimp Scampi

1. In a large skillet over medium heat, add half the butter and the shrimp. Cook for about 2 or 3 minutes and then flip over the shrimp. Add the garlic, Italian seasoning, and oregano, and cook for 2 or 3 more minutes. Transfer the shrimp to a plate, and set aside.

2. In a large pan, cook the linguine in boiling water according to the package directions. Drain, reserving about ½ cup pasta water, and set aside.

3. In the skillet, add the artichoke hearts, capers, Kalamata olives, anchovy paste, lemon juice, and the remaining butter. Bring to a simmer and then add the white wine and spinach. Cook for about 5 minutes or until the spinach is wilted and the alcohol flavor has cooked off.

4. Add the pasta water to the skillet, and mix until the sauce looks cohesive. Add the drained pasta and cooked shrimp, and toss.

5. Garnish with oregano, Parmesan, and lemon slices, and serve. Enjoy!

> **TIP**
>
> To elevate this dish or add a bit of extra protein, add some flaked leftover Weeknight Salmon (minus the dilly potatoes; see page 114) or some crumbled crispy prosciutto on top.

Grandma Mary's Homemade Pasta

1. Crack the eggs into a large bowl and beat them well with whisk.

2. Slowly start to add the flour to the bowl and gradually start mixing the flour with the eggs using a whisk or silicone spatula until the mixture is too sticky to keep adding more (about ¾ cup total).

3. Spread a ¼ cup of flour on the table or counter. Turn the sticky dough out onto your floured surface.

4. Begin kneading the dough with your hands only adding extra flour as needed (up to an ⅛ cup) until the dough is no longer sticky to the touch, about 5 to 10 minutes.

5. Form the kneaded dough into a ball and coat it lightly with oil. Add to a lightly oiled bowl, cover with a clean kitchen towel, and let it rest until you're ready to roll it out.

6. Spread the remaining ⅛ cup of flour on the table or counter and roll out the dough on your floured surface using a rolling pin or noodle stick. Turn the dough over a couple times while rolling and dust with a little flour as needed to avoid sticking to the surface until desired size and thickness, about ¼-inch thick.

7. Let the rolled out dough dry for half an hour (up to 1 hour), turning over halfway through. The dried texture should feel a little brittle.

8. Roll the dough up jelly roll-style and cut noodles to the desired width. Shake out the noodles and spread them onto a baking sheet to dry for another 30 minutes.

9. Bring a large pot of salted water to a boil. Add the noodles to water carefully and stir them gently. When the noodles rise to the top of the water, cook for 3 minutes longer. Drain the noodles after doing a taste test for doneness. Serve with your favorite sauce.

······· **TIPS** ·······

Sometimes I like to add a splash of
lemon juice or blanch the basil
before blending it to get an even
more green color.

If using a chunk of Parmesan, save
the rind for making soup or broth.

Spicy Pesto Pasta

This recipe is inspired by my love for pesto and all things spicy—as I'm writing this, I am just now realizing I may be addicted to pesto...and crushed red pepper flakes...and cheese in general...oh well!

The trick to making this dish great is the quality of the pesto you use. If you have the time and money, or can score a giant fresh basil supply from your mom's garden, I recommend making it from scratch (recipe follows).

1. In a large pan, cook the rigatoni pasta in boiling water according to the package directions.

2. In a separate large pan over medium heat, add the olive oil, garlic, crushed red pepper flakes, if using, and cherry tomatoes. Cook for about 5 minutes, but avoid browning the garlic.

3. Turn off the heat. Add the lemon juice, Parmesan, and Delishaas Pesto, and mix to combine. Mix in the heavy cream.

4. Add the cooked pasta directly from the water, draining most of the starchy water but leaving just enough to thicken the sauce, and toss to coat in the sauce. Turn on the heat to medium, and bring the pasta in the sauce up to a light simmer to lightly cook the heavy cream.

5. Garnish with torn pieces of burrata, crushed red pepper flakes, and fresh parsley, and serve with garlic knots to soak up all that saucy goodness. Enjoy!

Delishaas Pesto

1. In a small pan or skillet over low heat, cook the pine nuts, garlic, and shallot for a few minutes (no longer than 5 minutes).

2. Transfer the nuts and vegetables to a food processor. Add the basil, Parmesan, salt, extra virgin olive oil, and crushed red pepper flakes, and blend for about 4 or 5 minutes or until smooth.

3. Use immediately, or store any leftovers in an airtight container in the refrigerator for up to two weeks. Leave some breathing room in the container because the oil will thicken. Enjoy!

COMPLETE DISH
SERVES 3-4
PREP TIME: 5 MINUTES
TOTAL TIME: 30 MINUTES

PESTO
MAKES ABOUT 2 CUPS
PREP TIME: 5 MINUTES
TOTAL TIME: 10 MINUTES

1 pound (450g) rigatoni or spaghetti

3 tablespoons extra-virgin olive oil

8 garlic cloves, minced

1 teaspoon crushed red pepper flakes, plus extra for garnish (optional)

1 pint (10 ounces/285g) cherry tomatoes

Juice of ½ lemon

¼ cup grated Parmesan

3 ounces (85g) Delishaas Pesto or store-bought pesto

¼ cup heavy cream

1 x 8-ounce (226g) ball of burrata or fresh mozzarella

Handful of chopped fresh parsley, for garnish

Serve with

Frozen garlic knots, cooked according to package directions (optional)

For pesto

¾ cup pine nuts (or cashews, pistachios, or walnuts if pine nuts are insanely expensive)

6-8 garlic cloves, crushed

1 small shallot, roughly chopped

4 packed cups fresh basil

1 cup grated or roughly chopped Parmesan

½ teaspoon salt, or to taste

¾ cup good quality extra virgin olive oil

1 teaspoon crushed red pepper flakes (optional)

Special equipment

Food processor with the purée or chop blade attachment

Tomato Confit Orzo with Burrata

SERVES 3-4 | PREP TIME: 5 MINUTES | TOTAL TIME: 1 HOUR

I can't help but feel like a hopeless romantic with myself—self-care is important! Recipes like this one, and the rest of the pasta recipes in this chapter, are what I call "marry me meals," a playful way of saying you love and appreciate someone so much that you would marry them because they cooked such an incredible dish. Don't worry, being on the receiving end of this dish is not permanently binding. But let's not get it twisted—marriage is hard work, that of which I know nothing about. You're on your own for that one, kid! Love is love!

1. Starting by making the tomato confit: In a small pan over low heat, slowly cook the olive oil, grape tomatoes, crushed garlic, chili crisp, and basil for about 30 to 45 minutes, or until the tomatoes are a little blistered.

2. Meanwhile, in a large pan, cook the orzo in boiling water according to the package directions. Drain and set aside.

3. In a large skillet over medium-low heat, add the white onion and garlic paste, and sauté for 4 to 6 minutes or until translucent. Add the lemon juice and mustard, and mix until combined. Add the white wine and Parmesan, and mix again. Finally, add the parsley and artichoke hearts, and mix once more.

4. Add the orzo to the sauce, crack open the burrata and spread it all over the dish, followed by the tomato confit.

5. Season with salt and pepper, garnish with extra torn fresh basil, a drizzle of truffle oil, if using, and serve. Enjoy!

6–8 tablespoons olive oil

1 pint (10 ounces/285g) grape or cherry tomatoes

8 cloves garlic, crushed or thinly sliced

1 tablespoon chili crisp

4–5 basil leaves, plus extra for garnish

1 pound (450g) orzo

½ white onion

2 tablespoons of garlic or garlic paste

Juice of ½ lemon

1 tablespoon Dijon mustard

¼ cup dry white wine

¼ cup grated Parmesan

½ bunch fresh parsley, chopped

9 ounces (255g) jarred grilled artichoke hearts, quartered

2× 8-ounce (226g) ball of burrata, torn

Salt and freshly ground black pepper

Truffle oil (optional), for garnish

········· **TIP** ·········

When I'm finishing this pasta, I love going fishing in my fridge for veggies to add. It's incredibly tasty with asparagus!

3 tablespoons unsalted butter

4–5 garlic cloves, minced

1½ cups heavy cream

Salt and freshly ground black pepper

1 cup shredded Parmesan, plus extra for garnish

8 ounces (225g) baby bella mushrooms, thinly sliced

9 ounces (255g) canned artichoke hearts, drained

Handful of julienned sun-dried tomatoes

¼ cup cranberry sauce

1× 16-ounce (450g) package tortellini

Handful of roughly chopped fresh parsley or basil, for garnish

Tortellini Cranberry Alfredo

SERVES 4 | PREP TIME: 5 MINUTES | TOTAL TIME: 25 MINUTES

In my table-waiting days, I worked at a local Italian American restaurant that served this dish (no, it wasn't an Olive Garden), and the moment it touched my lips, I knew we would be together forever. This was one of the best sellers at the restaurant because I would recommend it to all my tables for its subtly sweet yet robust flavor combination. I just had to figure out how to make it myself. I know it sounds unusual, but think of it as tortellini with a tangy alfredo sauce—the cranberry is silent until you taste it and then it brightens up your whole palate. Game over, my friends. Just go ahead and make this one and thank me later. Sorry to be aggressive, but I love saying, "I told you so", when it comes to unusual food combinations.

.... **TIP** ....

If you want to add protein to this dish, grilled or rotisserie chicken are great options.

1. In a large pan over medium heat, cook the butter and garlic for 2 minutes or until the butter is melted.

2. Add the heavy cream, salt, pepper, and Parmesan, and stir. After about 5 minutes, when the mixture starts to bubble, add the mushrooms, and cook for 4 minutes. You don't want them to get mushy, so don't crowd the pan.

3. Add the artichoke hearts, sun-dried tomatoes, and cranberry sauce, and simmer, stirring occasionally, for 5 minutes.

4. In a large pan, cook the tortellini in boiling water according to the package directions. Drain and toss the tortellini in the sauce.

5. Garnish with Parmesan and parsley or basil, and serve. Enjoy!

Orecchiette with Spicy Italian Sausage & Spinach

SERVES 3-4 | PREP TIME: 10 MINUTES | TOTAL TIME: 30 MINUTES

**If you are someone like me, who grew up on Hamburger Helper, I think you'll be pleasantly surprised with this elevated version. Originally, I came up with this recipe in an attempt to dirty just one dish, because ya boy didn't have a dishwasher! You often see this combo served with broccoli rabe, but when I was developing it, I only had spinach. It worked perfectly as a substitute and is something I always have on hand. So this is my "what do we already have in the fridge?" budget-friendly version of this classic Italian dish.
I hope you enjoy it!**

1 tablespoon extra virgin olive oil

1 white onion, chopped

4 garlic cloves, minced

1 pound (450g) ground pork (or whatever protein you want)

½ tablespoon Italian seasoning

½ teaspoon dried basil

1 teaspoon cayenne pepper

1 teaspoon ground cumin

1 teaspoon fennel seeds

1 teaspoon sweet paprika

1 teaspoon crushed red pepper flakes (optional)

1 pound (450g) orecchiette

4 cups chicken or vegetable broth

½ bunch fresh parsley, finely chopped

2 handfuls of fresh spinach

¼ cup freshly grated Pecorino Romano

1. To a large pot or large skillet over medium heat, add the olive oil, onion, and garlic, and cook for 8 to 10 minutes or until it turns golden.

2. Add the ground pork, and begin to brown. Add the Italian seasoning, basil, cayenne pepper, cumin, fennel seeds, paprika, and crushed red pepper flakes, if using.

3. When the pork is browned, about 8 to 10 minutes, add the dry orecchiette.

4. Slowly pour in ⅓ of the chicken broth. Increase the heat to high, and bring to a boil, stirring occasionally to be sure nothing sticks to the bottom of the pan, and adding more broth as it cooks down. You'll feel it when things start to stick to the pan.

5. When the pasta is cooked, add the parsley and stir to combine. Add the spinach, and toss until wilted.

6. Garnish with Pecorino Romano, and serve. Enjoy!

2 tablespoons extra-virgin olive oil or unsalted butter

6-8 garlic cloves, minced

1 pint (10 ounces/285g) cherry tomatoes

1× 16-20-ounce (450-560g) package gnocchi

8 ounces (225g) canned artichoke hearts, drained and halved

2 tablespoons fresh oregano or 1 tablespoon dried oregano

½ teaspoon crushed red pepper flakes, plus extra for garnish

1½ teaspoons Italian seasoning

2 cups fresh spinach

½ teaspoon champagne vinegar (optional, if you like a little tang!)

2 cups homemade or store-bought vodka sauce

1× 12-ounce (340g) container marinated mozzarella, oil reserved for garnish

Handful of fresh basil, torn, for garnish

Serve with:

Cheesy garlic bread or a sliced fresh baguette

One-Pot Vodka Gnocchi

SERVES 3-4 | PREP TIME: 5 MINUTES | TOTAL TIME: 1 HOUR

When I'm hanging out with my friends, I always want to try out my new recipes on them. This is one tried-and-true recipe I love making for them because it's quick and delish so we can hop back into our video games and continue pwning noobs.

This dish is the all-time favorite of two of my best friends, Mary and Adam. Every time I go visit them in Fargo, Adam asks me to make it in bulk so he can eat it for a whole week! I love it because it's a one-pot dish, so cleanup is a breeze. Boooooo dishes! Yay pastaaa!

1. Preheat the oven to 350°F (180°C).

2. In a large skillet or oven-safe pot over medium heat, add the extra virgin olive oil, garlic, cherry tomatoes, and gnocchi, and cook for about 15 minutes, flipping the gnocchi every 5 minutes, until crisp and slightly brown on all sides.

3. Add the artichoke hearts, oregano, crushed red pepper flakes, and Italian seasoning, and let everything bloom for about 2 minutes.

4. Add the spinach, and cook for about 3 or 4 minutes or until wilted.

5. Add the champagne vinegar, if using, and the vodka sauce, and mix. Top with the marinated mozzarella and bake for 25 to 30 minutes.

6. Remove from the oven. Garnish with the reserved mozzarella oil, basil, and more crushed red pepper flakes, and serve. Enjoy!

Magic Conch Pasta

SERVES 4-6 | PREP TIME: 15 MINUTES | TOTAL TIME: 45 MINUTES

I love the unique shape of pasta shells! I'm obsessed with the ocean, and this pasta shells are known as the conch of the pasta world because of its Greek and Italian name, *conchiglie*. I like to call this recipe my "Magic Conch Pasta" because of the *SpongeBob SquarePants* episode in which SpongeBob and Patrick rely on and confide in a magic conch to solve all their problems. Likewise, this creamy, cheesy, lemony pasta, with summer vegetables and fresh herbs, seems to solve all my problems when I eat it.

1. Preheat the oven to 350°F (180°C).

2. In a large pan, cook the pasta shells in boiling water according to the package directions until just al dente (about 2 or 3 minutes before they're fully cooked). Drain and set aside.

3. In a large, oven-safe pan or skillet over medium heat, add the olive oil, onion, and shallots, and sauté for about 5 to 10 minutes or until the vegetables start to slightly brown. Add the lemon zest, lemon juice, salt, pepper, crushed red pepper flakes, Italian seasoning, oregano, and sun-dried tomato paste, and stir to combine.

4. Add the hot Italian sausage, and cook for 8 to 10 minutes or until browned.

5. Add the garlic, spinach, ricotta, and Parmesan, and mix until combined. Remove from the heat.

6. Spoon the filling into the shells, and set aside.

7. In the skillet or oven-safe pan, add the marinara sauce. Add the stuffed shells in whatever pattern you like. I usually make a circle.

8. Bake for 25 to 30 minutes or until the cheese starts to get a golden color. Begin checking for doneness at 25 minutes.

9. Remove from the oven. Garnish with more Parmesan, parsley, and crushed red pepper flakes, and serve. Enjoy!

12 ounces (340g) medium to jumbo pasta shells

1 tablespoon olive oil

1 yellow onion, finely chopped

3 shallots, thinly sliced

Zest and juice of 1 lemon

Salt and freshly ground black pepper

1 teaspoon crushed red pepper flakes, plus extra for garnish

1 teaspoon Italian seasoning

1 teaspoon fresh or dried oregano, roughly chopped

1× 6-7-ounce (170-200g) jar of sun-dried tomatoes with oil, puréed

1 pound (450g) hot Italian sausage (or mild if you don't like it spicy)

4-6 garlic cloves, minced

2 handfuls of spinach (about 2 cups)

1× 15-ounce (425g) container ricotta (any fat percentage)

3 ounces (85g) grated or shredded Parmesan, plus extra for garnish

1× 24-ounce (680g) jar marinara sauce of choice (I recommend Rao's)

Chopped fresh parsley, for garnish

Ingredients

1 pound (450g) sliced bacon (or less if you prefer)

1 pound pasta of choice (I use rigatoni because it catches the sauce well)

1 white or yellow onion, roughly chopped

4 garlic cloves

4 ounces (115g) cream cheese (about ½× 8-ounce/225g block), softened

1 cup chicken broth

2 cups shredded marble Jack or Colby Jack, divided

¼ cup heavy whipping cream

Salt and freshly ground black pepper

1 teaspoon onion powder

1 teaspoon garlic powder

1 teaspoon dried parsley

1 teaspoon dried dill

1 teaspoon dried chives

1 teaspoon Cajun seasoning

2 cups fresh spinach

½ rotisserie chicken, shredded into bite-size pieces

2 tablespoons hot sauce (I like Frank's RedHot), plus extra for garnish

½ bunch fresh parsley, chopped, for garnish

Serve with

1 loaf garlic bread or hot buttered bread of choice

TIP

This is another opportunity for snack bacon (see page 48)!

Buffalo Chicken Pasta

SERVES 4-6 | PREP TIME: 5 MINUTES | TOTAL TIME: 30 MINUTES

Buffalo chicken dip is something you absolutely can expect to see at any given potluck. Potlucks are a pretty common occurrence around the world, not just in the Midwest. They've always been seen as a great way to lessen the cooking load while also sharing. In this recipe, I'm turning the potluck's star dish into one of my other favorite things—pasta!

1. In a large, oven-safe pan or skillet over medium heat, cook the bacon for 10 to 15 minutes or until browned and crispy. Flip over the bacon, and cook for 10 more minutes. Transfer to a paper towel–lined plate, allow to cool, and then chop.

2. In a large pan, cook the pasta in boiling water according to the package directions. Drain and set aside.

3. Meanwhile, add the onion to the bacon fat in the pan, and cook for about 8 to 10 minutes or until translucent.

4. Add the garlic, cream cheese, chicken broth, half of the shredded cheese, and the heavy whipping cream, and stir to combine. Cook for 5 minutes or until the cream cheese has been incorporated and the cheese sauce is bubbling. Reduce the heat to low.

5. Add the salt, pepper, onion powder, garlic powder, parsley, dill, chives, and Cajun seasoning, and stir until combined. Add the spinach, chicken, and hot sauce, and mix again.

6. Preheat the broiler.

7. Toss the pasta in the chicken-cheese sauce. Top with the remaining shredded cheese and the chopped bacon.

8. Broil for 3 to 5 minutes or until the cheese is melted or starting to brown.

9. Remove from the oven. Top with more hot sauce and parsley, and serve with some garlic bread to soak up the sauce (thank me later!). Enjoy!

Cheesy Pumpkin Pasta

SERVES 4-6 | PREP TIME: 5 MINUTES | TOTAL TIME: 25 MINUTES

If fall was a pasta dish, this would be it. It feels like pulling on fuzzy socks; leaves changing colors; warm-colored sweaters with wide, heavy cable knits; and reading a book next to a fireplace with a warm beverage. This dish is pumpkin flavored but not in an overwhelming way; it's savory and cheesy and complex. Look out pumpkin spice...everything, your days are numbered. Pumpkin pasta is on its way to steal the title of favorite fall craving!

1 pound (450g) mini shell pasta (You can use whatever pasta you want, but I recommend one that will catch all the sauce)

3 tablespoons unsalted butter

1× 9-ounce (255g) can pumpkin purée

1× 5.2-ounce (150g) package Boursin (I like to use chives and shallots flavor)

1 teaspoon crushed red pepper flakes, plus extra for garnish

1 teaspoon dried rosemary

1 teaspoon fresh or dried oregano

1 teaspoon onion powder

Salt and freshly ground black pepper

½ cup Greek yogurt

Chili oil or spicy olive oil and chopped fresh parsley, for garnish

1. In a large pan, cook the mini shell pasta in boiling water according to the package directions. Drain, reserving ½ cup pasta water, and set aside.

2. In a large skillet over medium heat, melt the butter. Add the pumpkin purée and Boursin, and stir until combined.

3. Add the crushed red pepper flakes, rosemary, oregano, onion powder, salt, and pepper, and stir. Slowly pour in a little of the reserved pasta water, and stir until the cheese sauce is soft and fluffy. Give it a little taste test to check if it needs more salt and pepper.

4. Toss in the drained pasta, and stir to combine.

5. Add a few dollops of Greek yogurt and give everything a quick stir.

6. Garnish with a drizzle of chili oil or spicy oil, some parsley, and some extra crushed red pepper flakes, and serve. Enjoy!

CASSEROLES, HOT DISHES & OTHER MIDWEST-Y STUFF

My Mom's Tater Tot Hot Dish

SERVES 6–8 (BUT MAYBE DOUBLE THE BATCH IF I'M COMING OVER)
PREP TIME: 5 MINUTES | TOTAL TIME: 1 HOUR

My mama's tater tot hot dish is quite literally the pinnacle of Midwest cuisine, but I'm obviously biased when it comes to my mom's cooking. Think of this dish as a deconstructed cheeseburger in a way. I would often request this on my birthday because I loved it so much. And any time it was on the menu, my mom would have to make two pans—we would eat an entire pan for supper and then dig into the second pan for breakfast the next day!

This is a PERFECT weekend meal, it comes together with very little effort, and it's even more fun if you use different types of potatoes on top. When else, as an adult, would you buy tater tots that are shaped as letters or smiley faces?

- 1 pound (450g) ground beef (I use 90% lean, but use what you want or a ground plant-based protein of choice)
- 1 teaspoon salt, or to taste
- 1 teaspoon freshly ground black pepper, or to taste
- 1 teaspoon smoked paprika
- Healthy shake of Lawry's Seasoned Salt (about ½ tablespoon; optional)
- 1 red onion, chopped
- 5 garlic cloves
- 12 ounces (340g) frozen mixed vegetables
- 1× 10.5-ounce (300g) can cream of mushroom soup
- 32 ounces (950g) frozen tater tots
- 13 ounces (370g) frozen onion rings
- 16 ounces (450g) American cheese slices

1. Preheat the oven to 350°F (180°C).

2. In a medium pan over medium heat, add the ground beef and brown for about 6 minutes, breaking up the meat as it cooks. Add the salt, pepper, paprika and Lawry's Seasoned Salt and mix to combine.

3. Add the onion and garlic, and cook for about 12 minutes or until the vegetables have started to caramelize but aren't fully browned.

4. Use a slotted spoon to strain the meat from the fat in the pan, and transfer to a 9×13-inch (23×33cm) casserole dish.

5. Add the frozen mixed vegetables and the cream of mushroom soup to the meat, and stir to combine.

6. Arrange the frozen tater tots on top in a lined pattern, or go wild with another design. Arrange the onion rings on top of the tater tots.

7. Bake for 30 to 45 minutes. Look for crispy bits on the top of the taters and onion rings.

8. Remove from the oven, and add the slices of American cheese over the top to cover, and pop the dish back in the oven for 10 minutes.

9. Remove from the oven, and let sit for 10 minutes before serving because it's going to be hot AF. Enjoy!

Chicken Bacon Ranch Pot Pie

SERVES 4–6 | PREP TIME: 10 MINUTES | TOTAL TIME: 45 MINUTES

8 ounces (230g) bacon, roughly chopped

2 chicken breasts (about 32 ounces/907g total), roughly chopped into 1-inch (2.5cm) cubes

½ tablespoon sweet paprika

1 teaspoon ground cumin

Salt and freshly ground black pepper

1 small red onion, roughly chopped

2 carrots, sliced

2 celery stalks, roughly chopped

½ each red, orange, and yellow bell pepper, ribs and seeds removed and roughly chopped

4–6 garlic cloves, minced

½ cup sour cream

½ cup Homemade Ranch Dressing (see page 212) or store-bought ranch dressing

1 teaspoon crushed red pepper flakes (optional)

1× 16-ounce (453g) package frozen phyllo dough, at room temperature

4 tablespoons unsalted butter, melted

Fresh thyme, for garnish (optional)

I created this delightfully cozy dish when I was craving a homemade pot pie but didn't have the willpower to make dough or do much else. I wanted something warm and filling and homey, but also cute. I was cleaning out my freezer and noticed I had some phyllo. This is an exceptional way to get around using a pastry crust, and you don't have to trust me because you'll understand immediately when you make this. I thought to myself, *"What would Erin McDowell do?"* She probably would make her own crust, but she also would condone using phyllo in a pinch.

1. Preheat the oven to 350°F (180°C).

2. In a large oven-safe skillet or pan over medium heat add the bacon, and cook for 5 to 10 minutes or until halfway done.

3. Add the chicken and cook for 6 to 8 minutes per side until it's no longer pink.

4. Season with the paprika, cumin, salt, and pepper. Add the mirepoix (red onion, carrots, and celery) and the bell peppers, and cook for about 8 to 10 minutes or until they turn soft.

5. Add the garlic, sour cream, Homemade Ranch Dressing, and crushed red pepper flakes, if using. Stir well to coat.

6. Layer the phyllo dough on top, and drizzle or brush the butter over the phyllo.

7. Bake for 30 minutes (depending on how thawed your dough is) or until the crust is golden brown. Start checking at 20 minutes.

8. Garnish with thyme, and let cool for 8 to 10 minutes before serving. Enjoy!

> .... **TIP** ....
>
> You want to be sure your phyllo is ready to go, at room temperature, when you're ready to cook, so this is your friendly reminder to take it out of the freezer!

TV Dinner Hot Dish

SERVES 6-8 | PREP TIME: 10 MINUTES | TOTAL TIME: 45 MINUTES

I was a strange little kid, there's no doubt about that. We normally didn't buy frozen meals when I was growing up because they were expensive (and because my mom's a way better cook), oh, and to be honest, they never heated up fully in the oven, even when you followed the package instructions.

But I'm not coming for Kid Cuisine. On very special occasions, when I was on my best behavior and I was allowed to get a "treat" from the grocery store, I would pick either a frozen TV dinner or a family-sized bag of Old Dutch dill pickle chips and a Diet Coke. I really loved decorating the little treat that came with the frozen meal, and I got to eat it on a tray with my grandparents while we watched old movies.

Nowadays I'll still get down with a bag of dill pickle chips, but this is my tribute to classic TV dinners with my grandpa.

1. Prepare the chicken nuggets, if using, according to package instructions. If using a rotisserie chicken or other frozen, breaded chicken, shred or cut into chunks.

2. Preheat the oven to 350°F (180°C), if it's not already at that temperature from the chicken nuggets.

3. In a large pan over medium heat, add half the butter, the onion, and the bell pepper, and sauté for 6 to 8 minutes or until the onions start to slightly brown. Add the potatoes, salt, pepper, thyme, rosemary, and the remaining butter.

4. When the potatoes are starting to brown and crisp up, add the corn, cream of roasted mushroom and garlic soup, and half of the gravy, and stir until combined. Pour into a 9x13 (23×33cm) casserole dish.

5. Press some of the chicken nuggets into the mixture in the casserole dish so you'll get a little chicken in every bite. Top with Monterey Jack and the remaining chicken nuggets (this is going to get extra crispy) in whatever pattern your heart desires!

6. Bake for 25 to 30 minutes or until everything is bubbling with cheesy goodness.

7. Remove from the oven and let it sit for a few minutes because it's going to be pipin' hot. Garnish with chives, rosemary, and thyme, and serve with extra gravy or Homemade Ranch Dressing. Enjoy!

1× 21-ounce (600g) package frozen chicken nuggets, or ½ a rotisserie chicken, or other frozen breaded chicken

4 tablespoons unsalted butter, divided

1 white or yellow onion, roughly chopped

1 bell pepper (any color), ribs and seeds removed and roughly chopped

16 ounces (450g) diced frozen potatoes

Salt and freshly ground black pepper

1 teaspoon fresh or dried thyme, plus extra for garnish

1 teaspoon fresh or dried rosemary, plus extra for garnish

15 ounces (425g) corn, canned or fresh/frozen, drained if using canned

1× 10.5-ounce (300g) can creamy roasted mushroom and garlic soup (or whatever cream soup you prefer)

12 ounces (340g) jarred or homemade beef or chicken gravy, divided, plus extra for serving

1 cup shredded Monterey Jack or cheese of choice

Chopped fresh chives, for garnish

Serve with

Homemade Ranch Dressing (see page 212)

········ **TIPS** ·········

Treat yourself to something sweet, like a brownie, on the side. You deserve it.

Party Potato Casserole

SERVES 4–6 | PREP TIME: 10 MINUTES | TOTAL TIME: 1 HOUR

28-30 ounces (800–850g) frozen potatoes with peppers and onions, roughly thawed

1× 2-ounce (55g) package onion soup and dip mix

1 cup sour cream (any fat)

1 cup chicken broth or bone broth

2 cups shredded cheese of choice, divided

Salt and freshly ground black pepper

½ tablespoon Italian seasoning

1 teaspoon crushed red pepper flakes, plus more for garnish

Handful of kettle or wavy original flavor potato chips, roughly crushed (about ½ cup)

2 green onions, sliced

This take on a potato casserole is what some might refer to as "funeral potatoes." It's a Midwest tradition that when friends or neighbors have experienced a loss in the family, you check in and drop off food. It brings a real sense of community, especially when someone is going through a rough time. But in case you don't want to listen to "Funeral" by Phoebe Bridgers and eat this alone, I've decided to rename this dish Party Potato Casserole. It's a mix of funeral potatoes and scalloped potatoes all in one!

The loss of loved ones is so hard, but I love to find the light and think about all the wonderful things people taught us and all the amazing things we got to share with them! And I'm thankful I get to share all these recipes with you. So you can have these potatoes at any time, not just when you're sad. But most importantly! Life is a party, like these potatoes, let's celebrate it!

1. Preheat the oven to 350°F (180°C).

2. In a large bowl, combine the frozen potatoes, onion soup and dip mix, sour cream, chicken broth, most of the cheese, salt, and pepper. Transfer the mixture to a 9×13-inch (23×33cm) casserole dish, and bake for 45 minutes.

3. Remove from the oven. Add the Italian seasoning and crushed red pepper flakes, and mix well. Top with the remaining cheese, and sprinkle potato chips over the top.

4. Bake for 10 to 15 more minutes or until the cheese is melty and the chips have started to brown slightly.

5. Remove from the oven. Garnish with more crushed red pepper flakes if you'd like and sliced scallions. Let cool for 10 minutes before serving. Enjoy!

Tuna Casserole with Rye Chips

SERVES 6-8 | PREP TIME: 10 MINUTES | TOTAL TIME: 45 MINUTES

Tuna casserole is a tried-and-true American classic, to say the least! I have vivid memories of playing around outside with my siblings and the neighborhood kids and being called to the house because "DINNER'S READY!" Oh, and did I tell you we also used to have a giant bell in the shape of a chicken attached to the house that my parents would ring? All of us kids would come running in like cattle to wash up and sit down for dinner.

And although the traditional version is absolutely delicious, I wanted to add even more of my favorite flavors to dress it up. Rye chips are the best part of Gardetto's snack mix, and when they started selling them on their own, that's when I knew we, as a society, were going to be okay.

1. In a large pan, cook the pasta in boiling water according to the package directions. Drain and set aside.

2. In a large skillet over medium heat, melt the butter. Add the onion, frozen vegetables, and garlic, and cook for about 5 minutes. Add the broccoli cheese soup, salt, pepper, crushed red pepper flakes, Italian seasoning, and cumin, and stir.

3. Add the white cheddar and tuna, and stir until the cheese is entirely melted and the tuna is fully incorporated.

4. Transfer the pasta to a large casserole dish, top with the cheesy tuna mixture, and stir well to combine and coat. Top with more cheese if you want, which I always approve of.

5. Bake for 30 minutes.

6. In a small bowl, combine the melted butter, Parmesan, and rye chips.

7. Remove the casserole from the oven, cover with the chip topping, and pop it back in the oven for 10 more minutes.

8. Remove from the oven, and let cool for a couple minutes before garnishing with parsley and green onions and serving. Enjoy!

1 pound (450g) pasta of choice (egg noodles, rigatoni, or penne work best)

4 tablespoons unsalted butter, plus 2 tablespoons, melted

1 white or yellow onion, roughly chopped

1× 12-ounce (340g) bag frozen vegetables of choice (corn, green bean, carrots, or a mix)

3-4 garlic cloves, minced

1× 10.5-ounce (300g) can broccoli cheese soup

Salt and freshly ground black pepper

1 teaspoon crushed red pepper flakes

1 teaspoon Italian seasoning

1 teaspoon ground cumin

1-1½ cups shredded white cheddar cheese

2× 4.5-ounce (115g) cans premium tuna in oil or water (I prefer oil)

¼ cup grated Parmesan, divided

¼ cup rye chips, crumbled (or just use regular potato chips if you prefer)

Handful of fresh parsley, for garnish

3-4 green onions, sliced, for garnish

> **·········· TIP ··········**
>
> I am a huge cheerleader of freshly grating your cheese. Fresh isn't tossed in cornstarch like store-bought grated cheese is, and you'll notice it makes a difference in melty-ness, texture, and flavor.

Baked Mac & Cheese with Mini Corn Dogs

SERVES 4-6 | PREP TIME: 15 MINUTES | TOTAL TIME: 45 MINUTES

1 pound (450g) macaroni or other tubular pasta (ziti or rigatoni work great, too)

3 tablespoons unsalted butter

3 tablespoons minced garlic

2–3 tablespoons all-purpose flour

½ cup buttermilk

16 ounces (450g) freshly shredded cheddar

7 ounces (200g) freshly shredded Colby Jack

Salt and freshly ground black pepper

1 teaspoon sweet paprika

1 teaspoon onion powder

1 teaspoon ground mustard

½ teaspoon ground cayenne pepper (optional)

½ cup heavy cream

1× 32-ounce (950g) package frozen mini corn dogs, thawed

Honey or hot honey and sliced green onions, for garnish

Serve with

Mustard and ketchup, for dipping the doggies!

Not gonna lie, this is an excuse to enjoy another nostalgic popular craving I have. Whenever I eat hot dogs, I crave mac and cheese and vice versa, probably because I always had them paired together as a kid. Whenever I was eating Kraft, hot dogs were nearby. Adding a little bit of ketchup is apparently a hot topic for a lot of people. I like a little bit with some mac because it adds a hint of vinegary goodness. This recipe is for when I want to pretend to be sophisticated but also eat like I did as a kid.

1. Preheat the oven to 350°F (180°C).

2. In a large pot, cook the macaroni in boiling water according to the package directions. Drain and set aside.

3. In the same pot over low to medium heat, add the butter and garlic, and cook, stirring, for about 2 or 3 minutes or until combined and the butter has melted. Sprinkle in the flour, and stir to combine. Add the buttermilk, and stir until smooth.

4. Add the cheddar and Colby Jack to melt, along with the salt, black pepper, paprika, onion powder, ground mustard, and cayenne pepper (optional). Top with the heavy cream and stir to combine. When the cheese starts to melt and create strings, toss in the drained pasta. Season with salt and pepper, and stir.

5. Pour the cheesy pasta into a 9×13 (23×33cm) casserole dish, and top with an even layer of the mini corn dogs.

6. Bake for 25 to 30 minutes or until everything is golden brown.

7. Remove from the oven and let cook for 5 minutes. Garnish with honey and sliced green onions, and serve with mustard and ketchup for dipping. Enjoy!

Chicken Wild Rice Casserole

SERVES 4-6 | PREP TIME: 5 MINUTES | TOTAL TIME: 45 MINUTES

We grew up eating a lot of wild rice (and rice in general). We were also no strangers to Rice-A-Roni or Hamburger Helper when we were looking for a quick meal to feed our large family.

I love utilizing a rotisserie chicken any chance I get, and as usual, this recipe combines some of my favorite nostalgic dishes to make them even better. You can add any vegetables you'd like, too. Try adding frozen mixed veggies or a stuffing mix. You'll be pleasantly surprised!

1. Preheat the oven to 350°F (180°C).

2. Prepare the wild rice and orzo according to the package instructions. Set aside.

3. In a large skillet over medium to high heat, heat the olive oil and butter. Add the carrots, celery, onion, and garlic. Season well with salt and pepper. Cook for 6 to 8 minutes or until the onion is translucent. Don't burn the garlic.

4. Add the mushrooms, crushed red pepper flakes, and Italian seasoning, and cook for about 6 to 8 minutes. Add the all-purpose flour on top to coat everything evenly.

5. Begin incorporating the chicken broth (don't add it all at once), continuing to stir. When the mixture is creamy, add more broth. Bring to a simmer, and add the wild rice and orzo.

6. Transfer everything to a 9×13 (23×33cm) casserole dish, and mix in the shredded chicken, thyme, and heavy cream, give it a good mix to make sure everything is evenly disturbed.

7. Bake for 20 minutes. After 10 minutes, give it a stir to be sure everything is absorbing properly.

8. Remove from the oven. Garnish with fresh parsley and as much Parmesan as you can handle, and serve. Enjoy!

2 cups wild rice

1 cup orzo

2 tablespoons olive oil

2 tablespoons unsalted butter

2 carrots, roughly chopped

2 celery stalks, roughly chopped

1 white or yellow onion, chopped

6-8 garlic cloves, minced

Salt and freshly ground black pepper

8 ounces (225g) baby bella mushrooms, thinly sliced

1 teaspoon crushed red pepper flakes

½ tablespoon Italian seasoning

2 tablespoons all-purpose flour

3 cups low-sodium chicken or vegetable broth

½ rotisserie chicken, shredded

6 sprigs of thyme

½ cup heavy cream

Fresh parsley and grated Parmesan, for garnish

> **TIP**
>
> This can also be made in a 5-quart (4.5 liter) slow cooker by adding everything to the slow cooker, covering, and cooking on low for 3 or 4 hours.

Eggplant Rollatini

SERVES 3-4 | PREP TIME: 20 MINUTES | TOTAL TIME: 1 HOUR

1-2 eggplants, tops removed and sliced about ¼ inch (6mm) thick from top to bottom (not rounds)

Kosher salt

1× 15-ounce (425g) container ricotta (any fat percentage)

1 tablespoon garlic powder

1 tablespoon onion powder

1 tablespoon Italian seasoning

1 egg (optional, for optimal binding, but not necessary)

¼ cup grated Parmesan, plus extra for garnish

Juice of ½ lemon

1 cup fresh spinach

24 ounces (680g) marinara sauce

4 ounces (115g) shredded mozzarella

½ cup chopped fresh parsley, for garnish

1 pound (450g) hot, cooked spaghetti or angel hair pasta

Eggplant gets a bad rap. I believe it's because of the emoji. We're throwing too much disrespect on the vegetable itself.

When I was vegetarian for a short year, I basically lived off this dish (and a heck ton of salads and veggie sandwiches). It just hits the spot so right. I'm not going to lie, I would even eat it directly out of the fridge.

This recipe takes a little bit longer to make than some others, but I find it very therapeutic. When I worked at Target, I would make this in bulk and bring it to all my vegetarian coworkers. It was a fun little party!

1. Preheat the oven to 250°F (120°C).

2. Spread the sliced eggplant on a rimmed baking sheet, and sprinkle both sides of each slice with salt. Bake for 10 minutes per side. Pat dry both sides of each slice with a paper towel and remove any remaining salt to prevent the dish from being too salty.

3. Increase the oven temperature to 350°F (180°C).

4. In a medium bowl, combine the ricotta, garlic powder, onion powder, Italian seasoning, and the egg, if using. Add the Parmesan, lemon juice and spinach , then stir to combine. If the mixture is too dry, add just a little bit of olive oil. You want it a little bit wet, a little bit *chaunky*, but easy to spoon.

5. Spoon the ricotta mixture down the center of each slice of eggplant. Depending on the size of the eggplant, start with 2 tablespoons filling per slice; if it's a larger eggplant, use about 3 or 4 tablespoons instead. Beginning at the cut top end, roll the eggplant down, over the filling, toward the bottom of the slice, keeping the roll tight so the filling stays inside. Repeat with the remaining slices.

6. Add half the marinara sauce to the bottom of a 9×13-inch (23×33cm) casserole dish. Add the eggplant rolls on top of sauce in a single layer to line the dish. Top with the mozzarella.

7. Bake for 30 minutes or until the cheese is melted or about to start bubbling/browning.

8. Remove from the oven. Garnish with parsley, and serve on top of the hot, cooked pasta with the remaining marinara sauce and a sprinkle of extra Parmesan. Enjoy!

> ········· **TIP** ·········
>
> If you are Type A and need the slices to be perfect, try using a mandoline slicer. But please please please be very careful not to injure yourself. I know many a chef and carpenter who have some really not-fun stories about sharp tools! But your slices will come out thin.

Cabbage Roll Casserole

SERVES 4-6 | PREP TIME: 30 MINUTES | TOTAL TIME: 1 HOUR 15 MINUTES

This recipe is inspired by the Polish part of my family. Because my mom is a saint, when she would plan out dinners each week, she would ask my dad what he was craving. He would always request meat and potato–type recipes, like this casserole. I'm not kidding when I tell you that this man was made for frigid winters. Residing in the upper Midwest, we need food that sticks to our bones because that's all you're going to have left when "winter is coming." (Yes, this will be my only reference to *Game of Thrones* in this book.) This dish might not be as visually appealing as some, but I promise it will make the clean plate *clurb*.

1. Preheat the oven to 350°F (180°C).

2. Bring a large pot of salted water to a boil over medium-high heat (just like you would for pasta). Add the cabbage, stem side down and boil for 3 or 4 minutes. Using tongs, transfer the cabbage to a colander to drain and cool.

3. Peel off the large cabbage leaves. Flip over each leaf so you can see the ribs, and cut the large rib out of the center of each leaf so the cabbage can bend a little easier. Set aside.

4. Combine the Italian sausage, ground beef, onion, shallot, garlic, carrots, celery, and rice in a large mixing bowl and season with salt and pepper. Add the mixture to a large pan over medium heat, add the olive oil and Cook for 8 to 10 minutes. Add the San Marzano tomatoes, with juice, followed by the egg and half of the dill and half of the parsley. Stir to combine.

5. To assemble, on one side of each cabbage leaf, add 3 or 4 tablespoons of filling. Fold the edges in, over the filling, and roll into a small burrito shape. Set on a platter, and repeat with remaining cabbage leaves and filling.

6. Pour half of the tomato sauce into the bottom of a 9×13-inch (23×33cm) casserole dish. (You might need a second dish depending on the depth of your dish.) Arrange the cabbage rolls on top of the tomato sauce in a single layer, followed by more sauce. Cover the pan with foil. (If the pan is very full, I recommend baking this on a baking sheet to prevent it dripping in the oven.)

7. Bake for 30 to 45 minutes. You'll know it's done when it looks like a lovely roast; the rolls will be nice and plump.

8. Remove from the oven, and let cool for 10 minutes before serving because that MF'er is going to be hot. Garnish with the remaining dill and parsley, and serve. Enjoy!

1 large head of cabbage, stem removed

2 tablespoons olive oil

1 pound (450g) Italian sausage, or 1 pound (450g) ground pork, dark meat chicken, or turkey, seasoned with 1 tablespoon Italian seasoning

½ pound (225g) lean ground beef, or 2× 10-ounce (285g) packages firm tofu, drained and crumbled

1 large white or yellow onion, or 1 bunch green onions, roughly chopped

1 shallot, minced

4-5 garlic cloves, minced

2 carrots, minced

2 celery stalks, finely chopped

1 cup uncooked jasmine rice

½ tablespoon kosher salt, or to taste

½ tablespoon freshly ground black pepper, or to taste

1× 28-ounce (800g) can diced San Marzano tomatoes, with juice

1 egg (omit if making vegan)

½ bunch fresh dill, roughly chopped, divided into 2 piles

1 bunch fresh parsley, roughly chopped and divided into 2 piles

1× 14-ounce (400g) jar tomato sauce

········· **TIPS** ·········

This is wonderful served with roasted vegetables, any kind of potato situation, or sauerkraut.

Said in a *Sling Blade* voice, "These may not be the prettiest dang things you've ever seen, but they are awful pretty eatin.'"

2 tablespoons unsalted butter

2 tablespoons olive oil

1 white or yellow onion, finely chopped

1½ pounds (680g) cooked chicken, cut into bite-sized pieces

4-5 garlic cloves

2 teaspoons ground cumin

1 teaspoon sweet paprika

Salt and freshly ground black pepper

1 tablespoon Italian seasoning

1½ cups Arborio rice

1× 10.5-ounce (300g) can cream of broccoli soup

5.2 ounces (225g) Boursin (try the garlic and herb)

1 head of broccoli, cut into florets

2 cups chicken broth

Shredded cheese of choice, crushed red pepper flakes, and chopped fresh parsley, for garnish (optional)

Special equipment

Meat thermometer

Chicken & Broccoli Bake

SERVES 4–6 | PREP TIME: 5 MINUTES | TOTAL TIME: 45 MINUTES

This is another classic hot dish we're known for in these parts. This recipe is based on my mom's classic casserole, but with the addition of a couple slightly elevated ingredients.

I hope the hot dishes and casseroles in this chapter will be extremely handy in your home, too, as a way to save some money and get something good in your tummy. Once you've mastered the basics of the hot dish, you'll see that you can put just about anything in a casserole dish! It's also incredibly handy for using up leftovers you don't want to go to waste. Then you can also argue the question, "is it a hotdish or a casserole?!"

1. Preheat the oven to 350°F (180°C).

2. In a large pan over medium heat, heat the butter and olive oil. When the butter is melted, add the onion, and cook for 4 to 6 minutes. Add the chicken, garlic, cumin, paprika, salt, pepper, and Italian seasoning, and stir to combine. Cook for 8 to 10 minutes.

3. In a 9×13-inch (23×33cm) casserole dish, pour in the dry Arborio rice. Add the chicken-onion mixture, followed by the cream of broccoli soup, Boursin, broccoli, and chicken broth, and stir to evenly combine. It's going to look a little soupy; that's how you want it for now.

4. Bake for 20 minutes.

5. Remove from the oven, give it a stir, and pop it back in the oven for 20 more minutes.

6. After it has baked for 40 minutes, remove from the oven and top with cheese and crushed red pepper flakes, if using. If not, keep baking for the last 5 minutes. Let rest for 5 to 10 minutes before serving because it's going to be very hot. Enjoy!

3

SOUPS, SALADS & LOVE TRIANGLES (A.K.A PIZZA)

LOVE

The meaning of love can vary wildly from person to person. People write about it, sing about it—it's a shared experience that we all as humans have together. I could make a list of all the things I love, and that would be a book in itself—I love my dog, my friends, and my family; I love whales and most things related to the ocean; and I love plants, video games, and pickles. And it's worth noting that we cannot control what or who we love and don't love. It's just part of who we are.

But sometimes the hardest thing to do is find love for yourself. Reportedly, Lizzo says "I love you" to herself every day, and I would do anything that woman asked of me. That doesn't make the practice any easier to follow, though. I have days when I want to sit in my feelings (which is totally an important and valid thing to do) and lie in bed all day with my dog and watch TV. There are times when I still find it hard to motivate myself and prioritize my mental health and safety or even cook for myself!

Sometimes I try to picture myself in a fantastical Marvel-type universe (and in none of them do I have crime-fighting skills or powers), where various timelines exist but where alternate versions of me lead different lives based on choices I could have made. I try to think of what the BEST version of me would do, and most of the time he's not lying in bed ordering takeout—BUT sometimes he is.

Food is healing and often a gateway to a greater conversation. We have the power to share what we love with so many people, celebrating traditions, birthdays, barbecues, reunions, funerals, travel, and more. Food makes us feel happy and sad. Food makes us powerful when it fuels our body for activity and our mind for change. I love food, and I love you.

SIDE SALADS & GREEN THINGS

Pink (Fruit) Salad

SERVES 4 | PREP TIME: 5 MINUTES | TOTAL TIME: 5 MINUTES

I love watermelon. I would eat an entire watermelon for breakfast if my stomach would allow it. Whenever I think of watermelon, I imagine a sunny day and cute little kid with a giant slice—bigger than their head!—eating around the seeds. My family feels the same about fresh fruit! We always had this fruit salad on the boat, along with fruit dip, when we were at the lake. Some cheeseball puffs, too. We also made a variation of this salad that featured different melons (depending on what was on sale) and kiwi. And, not to brag, but this recipe was my first featured salad on *Good Morning America*! Enjoy!

1 personal watermelon, cut into small pieces (see Tips)

1 pint (285g) strawberries, cut into bite-sized pieces

1 pint (245g) raspberries

1 cup cherries, fresh (pitted if fresh), frozen (thawed halfway if frozen), or dried

1 lime, half zested and juiced and half cut into wedges, for serving

2 tablespoon of honey or hot honey (optional)

1 or 2 pinches of flaky salt

2 tablespoons of fresh mint (optional, but recommended)

1. In a large bowl, combine the watermelon, strawberries, raspberries, and cherries.

2. Add the lime zest, lime juice, honey, if using, flaky salt, and mint, if using, and mix well again.

3. Store in an airtight container in the refrigerator until ready to serve. Enjoy!

TIPS

"Personal" watermelons are those cute little melons that are about 3 to 4 pounds (1–2kg) and 4 to 6 inches (10–15cm) in diameter. They're the perfect size if you can find one, or use half of a regular-size watermelon and eat the rest.

After the salad has been eaten, there's going to be a ton of flavorful juice left in the bowl. Use it to make a delicious beverage! Add the leftover juice to a pitcher, pour in double the amount of sparkling water, and add liquor of choice if you'd like. (Vodka is always a safe bet! But I bet you'd also enjoy it with tequila!)

This recipe is pretty adaptable. Try adding Tajín or some feta for even more flavor! But if you add feta, maybe don't use the leftover juice for a beverage.

For the salad

5 ounces (140g) arugula or mixed greens

1 blood orange, zested, peeled, and cut into rounds

1 grapefruit, peeled and cut into rounds

1 navel orange, peeled and cut into rounds

2× 4-ounce (225g) ball burrata, or 8 ounces (225g) of mini mozzarella balls

Pinch of salt

Pinch of freshly ground black pepper

Chopped fresh basil or mint, for garnish

For the dressing

1 shallot, minced

4-5 tablespoons extra virgin olive oil

1 tablespoon white balsamic vinegar or champagne vinegar

1 tablespoon honey or hot honey

Zest of 1 blood orange

Citrus Salad

SERVES 2–4 | PREP TIME: 10 MINUTES | TOTAL TIME: 15 MINUTES

This is a great recipe to start working on your knife skills, so you can get a little practice cutting ingredients like a pro. Not to mention, it's delicious year-round. I love this during the summer, when I get to use fresh mint and basil from the garden. It's equally good for using up winter citrus.

1. On a serving platter or in a large bowl, make a bed of arugula and top with the blood orange rounds, grapefruit rounds, and orange rounds arranged in any pattern you'd like. Tear the burrata and distribute on top.

2. In a small bowl, whisk together the dressing ingredients.

3. Pour the dressing over the salad, and toss to combine.

4. Garnish with a sprinkle of salt, pepper, and fresh basil, and serve. Enjoy!

Frog's Eye Salad

SERVES 8–10 | PREP TIME: 20 MINUTES | TOTAL TIME: 20 MINUTES (PLUS 3 HOURS FOR CHILLING OR UP TO OVERNIGHT FOR BEST RESULTS)

We've all gathered here with the knowledge that I was a weird little kid—I loved action figures, I loved sewing, I loved filling out all the things in my *Boy Scout Handbook*, and I loved this salad. You are going to come after me when I explain this one, and I know how it sounds. But essentially, for this recipe, you are boiling pasta, rinsing it, letting it soak in pineapple juice, and then tossing it with Cool Whip and fruit. It's a cold dessert pasta salad, and I love it. The name is a little repulsive, in my opinion, but I dont make the rules, it's fun for kids...and me.

½ box acini di pepe pasta (about 1 cup)

½ cup sugar

1½ tablespoons all-purpose flour or cornstarch

Pinch of salt

1× 20-ounce (560g) can pineapple tidbits (or crushed pineapple) with juice

1 large egg

Juice of ½ lemon

1× 20-ounce (560g) can pineapple chunks or tidbits, drained

1× 15-ounce (425g) can mandarin oranges, drained

¼ cup maraschino cherries

¼ cup sweetened shredded coconut, plus extra for garnish

1× 8-ounce (225g) container frozen whipped topping, thawed

1 cup rainbow marshmallows

1. In a large pan, cook the acini di pepe pasta in boiling water according to the package directions. Drain and rinse the pasta, and set it aside in a large bowl to cool or pop it in the refrigerator to cool faster.

2. In a small saucepan over medium heat, add the sugar, flour, salt, pineapple tidbits with juice, egg, and lemon juice. Bring to a simmer, and cook, stirring continuously, for about 6 to 8 minutes. Remove from the heat, and set aside to cool, or pop it in the fridge to cool faster.

3. When the pasta and pineapple liquid have cooled completely, add the pineapple liquid to the pasta. Return the bowl to the fridge for 1 hour to marinate.

4. Remove the bowl from the refrigerator. Add the pineapple chunks, mandarin oranges, and maraschino cherries, and toss so it's one strange-looking pasta. Add the coconut and whipped topping, and stir until everything is coated.

5. Transfer the salad to a serving bowl, and return it to the fridge until you're ready to serve.

6. Just before serving, add the rainbow marshmallows so they don't get soggy. Enjoy!

> ·········· **TIP** ··········
>
> This can be made with a fruit cocktail mix in place of the mandarin oranges. Just be sure to drain it well.

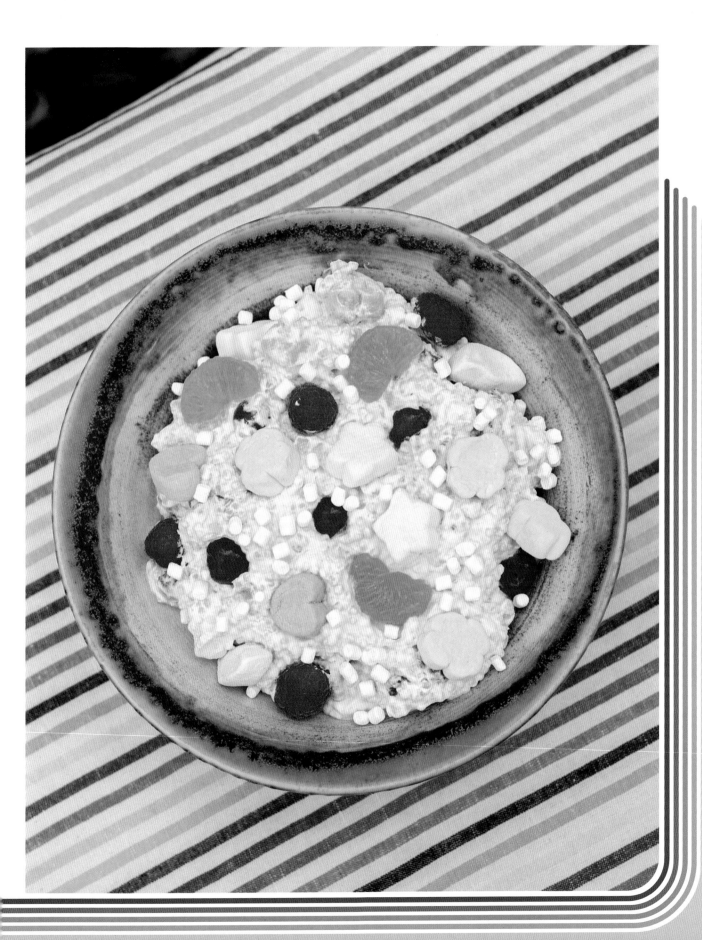

For the crust

2 cups crushed pretzels (large twists preferred)

¼ cup granulated sugar

8 tablespoons unsalted butter, melted

For the filling

4 ounces (115g) cream cheese (about ½× 8-ounce/225g block), softened

4 ounces (115g) frozen whipped topping, thawed (about ½× 8-ounce/225g container), plus extra for serving

½ cup confectioners' sugar

1 teaspoon vanilla extract

1× 6-ounce (170g) package strawberry gelatin mix

1½ cups fresh or frozen strawberries, chopped

Special equipment

9–10-inch (23–25cm) pie dish

Electric hand mixer

TIPS

You can make this pie with any of your favorite fruits and gelatin flavors.

If you let this pie sit for too long in the refrigerator (like a couple days), the pretzels can get a little soggy. It's best eaten fresh.

Strawberry & Pretzel Salad Pie

SERVES 6–8 | PREP TIME: 10 MINUTES | TOTAL TIME: 10 MINUTES (PLUS 3 HOURS SETTING TIME)

Salads look different wherever we are in the world, This is an example of another classic Midwest dessert salad. This dish is often made on a sheet pan for a large crowd because it's so easy to scale up. My family typically eats it during the summer because it's a chilled dessert that's great for a hot day. Most people in the Midwest will know exactly what this is because it's great for sharing and most likely to be found in any church bake sale or potluck.

The Midwest also is known for its gelatin consumption, which is fun. It's believed that back in the medieval days, gelatin was a way to identify wealth. When Scandinavian immigrants came to America, they brought with them their traditional ways of making gelatin. Can you guess what I'm going to say next? They brought that specialty to potlucks and church gatherings for easy dishes to share! So, to the Scandis, thanks for bringing Jell-O with ya. We love it!

1. Preheat the oven to 350°F (180°C). Lightly coat the pie dish with cooking oil spray.

2. In a medium bowl, combine the crushed pretzels, granulated sugar, and butter. Pour the pretzel mixture into the pie dish, and press it into an even layer to create a crust.

3. Bake for 10 minutes. Remove from the oven, and let it cool to room temperature.

4. For the filling, in a separate medium bowl, whisk together the cream cheese, whipped topping, confectioners' sugar, and vanilla extract until smooth. Or blend using an electric mixer on medium to high so its all combined.

5. Pour the cream cheese mixture into the pie crust, and spread it across the bottom and the sides of the crust to work as a sealant for the gelatin. Chill for 1 hour in the refrigerator.

6. Meanwhile, in a small bowl, whisk together the strawberry gelatin mix and 1 cup boiling water until dissolved. Set aside to cool in the fridge for the remainder of the hour.

7. When the gelatin has cooled but is still liquid-y, add the chopped strawberries, and pour on top of the pie's cream cheese layer. Let chill in the refrigerator for 3 hours.

8. Just before serving, top with big dollops of whipped topping, and serve. Enjoy!

Caramel Apple Twix Salad

SERVES 6-8 | PREP TIME: 5 MINUTES | TOTAL TIME: 15 MINUTES (PLUS 1 HOUR CHILLING TIME)

This recipe is a prime example of a "traditional" Midwestern church basement salad (it's also great for barbecues and honestly any time!), but I've tweaked it a little to modernize it and make it my own. Often this is known as Snickers salad because it uses Snickers bars, but I like to use Twix bars instead. I added some apples to sneak some fresh fruit into the mix and yield a really lovely crunch.

1 cup raw walnuts or nut of choice (optional)

1× 3.4-ounce (96g) package vanilla pudding mix

1 cup milk of choice

3 apples of choice, diced and divided (I like a combination of Honeycrisp and Granny Smith)

2 dashes of ground cinnamon

1× 8-ounce (225g) container frozen whipped topping or Cocowhip, thawed

5 ounces (140g) Twix candy bars, roughly chopped

Caramel sauce, for drizzling (optional)

1. In a dry skillet over low heat, toast the walnuts, if using, for 4 to 6 minutes until fragrant and lightly brown. Set aside.

2. In a large bowl, whisk together the vanilla pudding mix and milk until combined.

3. Stir in two-thirds of the diced apples along with, a dash of cinnamon, toasted walnuts, and whipped topping, and mix. Place in the refrigerator, and let it set up for at least 1 hour.

4. When ready to serve, mix in the remaining apple, the remaining dash of cinnamon, and the Twix (the best part), and drizzle with caramel sauce, if using. Enjoy!

- 1× 3.4-ounce (96g) package vanilla cheesecake pudding mix
- 1 cup buttermilk
- 1× 8-ounce (225g) container frozen whipped topping, thawed
- ½ cup blackberries or raspberries
- ½ cup blueberries
- ½ cup strawberries, cut into quarters
- 1× 20-ounce (560g) can crushed pineapple, drained
- 1-2 kiwis, roughly chopped
- 6 ounces (170g) graham crackers (6 whole crackers), Biscoff cookies, or shortbread Girl Scout cookies

Special equipment

Electric hand mixer

TIPS

The fruits used in this salad are interchangeable, so use whatever you prefer. You could use fruit pie filling in place of the fresh fruits. (That would be real frickin' naughty of you.)

If you want to keep this a little tra-dish, dip some cookies and into melted chocolate, to make them fudge stripe cookie–esque!

Fruit Tart Cookie Salad

SERVES 8–10 | PREP TIME: 10 MINUTES | TOTAL TIME: 15 MINUTES (PLUS 30 MINUTES FOR CHILLING)

Remember when I said that not all salads are green? Well, here you go. Salads come in all colors, shapes, and sizes, and vary by location. This one happens to be a dessert salad. A very healthy handful of the recipes in this book are based on things my mom would make, but this one is dedicated to her. She LOVES fruit pizza and tart pastries, so I pounced on the opportunity to make this Fruit Tart Cookie Salad just for her. Enjoy your tart pudding—I mean, cookie salad!

1. In a medium bowl, whisk together the pudding mix and buttermilk until smooth and thick. Or blend using an electric mixer on low to medium .

2. Add the whipped topping on top of the pudding mixture, and use a spatula to cut down into the bowl and gently scoop the pudding mixture back on top. Fold a few more times until everything is just incorporated.

3. Gently fold in the blackberries, blueberries, strawberries, and the pineapple. Cover and let the mixture chilll in the refrigerator for at least 30 minutes before serving.

4. When ready to serve, top with the crumbled graham crackers or cookies. (Don't do this ahead of time or they'll get soggy.) Enjoy!

Dill Pickle Salad

SERVES 4-6 | PREP TIME: 10 MINUTES | TOTAL TIME: 10 MINUTES

The first day I met one of my now best friends, Anna, we were preparing for a catering event that I was also helping host. While prepping, we discovered our shared love of pickles, Lizzo, handsome men, and the Midwest. If she wasn't busy saving the world as a physical therapist in women's pelvic health, I would spend every day with Anna in the kitchen. With this recipe, she and I came together to create something we both love.

This is a high-quality salad inspired by the grocery store kits that you might buy when you need a quick lunch. For the people who love pickles, I think you will really appreciate this one. You can add meat and cheese if you like. I recommend pepperoni or salami.

1. In a medium bowl, whisk together all the dressing ingredients except the olive oil. Slowly drizzle in the olive oil while whisking to emulsify the dressing. Set aside.

2. In a large serving bowl, add all salad ingredients. Pour the dressing over the salad, and toss to combine.

3. Garnish with dill and serve. Enjoy!

For the dressing

1× 1-ounce (30g) packet ranch salad dressing and seasoning mix

2 tablespoons mayonnaise

½ bunch fresh dill, roughly chopped, plus extra for garnish

Siracha, to taste (I use ½ tablespoon.)

¼–½ cup pickle brine (start with ¼ cup and add more to taste)

2 tablespoons olive oil. (I recommend a good quality olive oil if possible.)

For the salad

3–4 ounces (85–115g) mixed greens of choice

½ cup shredded carrots

A few handfuls of fresh green beans, chopped

½ red onion, chopped

3 scallions, chopped

5 dill pickles, dried with a paper towel and then cut into coins

¼ small green cabbage, chopped (optional)

⅓ cup cauliflower florets, roughly chopped

For the salad

3 ounces (85g) prosciutto (optional)

5 ounces (140g) salad greens, such as spinach or arugula

8 ounces (225g) cottage cheese or burrata, torn

15 ounces (425g) fresh or canned mandarin oranges, peeled if fresh and drained if canned

1½ cups blueberries or strawberries

4-6 fresh or dried figs, cut in half

Handful of mixed olives, sliced (28g) (optional)

For the dressing

2 tablespoons honey

3 tablespoons extra virgin olive oil

Salt and freshly ground black pepper

1 tablespoon jam of choice (I like to use fig jam for this; optional)

Salad for a Cutie

SERVES 2–4 | PREP TIME: 5 MINUTES | TOTAL TIME: 10 MINUTES

When you were a little kid, did you have a favorite snack? Maybe Dunkaroos or ants on a log? Mine was cottage cheese with canned mandarin oranges and a little salt and pepper because it was one of my mom's favorite childhood snacks. I received a lot of strange looks for this. I decided to use that strange and wonderful snack as an inspiration for this salad, with a few new updates. So hopefully you'll like this, too!

1. If you are using prosciutto, preheat the oven to 350°F (180°C), and line a baking sheet with parchment paper.

2. Arrange the slices of prosciutto on the baking sheet, and roast for 15 to 20 minutes or until crispy. Remove from the oven and set aside.

3. In a large bowl, add the salad greens, followed by the cottage cheese, mandarin oranges, blueberries, figs, and olives. Top with the crispy prosciutto.

4. In a small bowl, whisk together the dressing ingredients. Pour the dressing over the salad, and serve. Enjoy!

Chopped Ramen Salad

SERVES 4–6 AS | PREP TIME: 10 MINUTES | TOTAL TIME: 45 MINUTES (PLUS 2–3 HOURS OR MORE FOR CHILLING)

This dish was introduced to me at my Grandma Geneva's lake house, when we were all fartin' around in the kitchen preparing a lake lunch. Before this point, I had never had ramen. My cousin showed me all the wonderful ways instant ramen could be made while my aunt was making this dish. And let me tell you, this salad was a game-changer. Like most children, I wasn't too terribly fond of green things at that point. I was a vegetable eater, but that's only because I didn't have control over what my parents put on my plate. That, my friends, is where this salad comes in. It will make even the most cautious of vegetable eaters a salad STAN.

1. In a small bowl, whisk together all the dressing ingredients.

2. In a large serving bowl, combine all the salad ingredients.

3. Pour the dressing over the salad, and toss to combine. Pop the salad in the refrigerator for 2 or 3 hours or until you're ready to serve. This will soften the noodles the perfect amount for crunchy bites in your salad!

4. Garnish with a drizzle of Sriracha and some scallions, and serve. Enjoy!

For the dressing

2 tablespoons honey

1 teaspoon rice wine vinegar

1 tablespoon diluted black vinegar or apple cider vinegar

2 tablespoons soy sauce or coconut aminos

2 teaspoons sesame oil

Juice of ½ lemon

4 tablespoons garlic-infused olive oil

For the salad

¼ head of green or red cabbage, finely chopped

3 Persian cucumbers, finely chopped

1 cup shredded or matchstick carrots

1 head of romaine lettuce, roughly chopped

3 green onions, finely chopped, plus extra for garnish

1 celery stalk, finely sliced

1 red onion, finely chopped

1× 3-ounce (85g) package ramen, crumbled (seasoning package removed)

½ bunch fresh cilantro (optional)

Sriracha, for garnish

TIPS

All ramen works for this. I generally like to stick to the Sapporo Ichiban brand. They make gluten-free noodles, too!

Serve this salad with chips to make it a salsa-like dip.

Depending on the type of noodle flavor you buy, use the leftover seasoning packet like a chicken bouillon seasoning the next time you want to bump up the flavor or something.

Remember, not everyone loves cilantro—to some people it tastes like soap! So maybe leave it on the side so people can garnish with it if they like.

4-5 ounces (115-140g) arugula

2 Persian cucumbers, cut into quarters or ribbons

½ cup shelled walnuts or pistachios (optional)

6 ounces (170g) prosciutto (I cut the slices in half to make more wraps)

1 medium peach or nectarine, cut into thin slices

4 ounces (115g) goat cheese, divided into ½-tablespoon dollops, use any extra for serving

Juice of ½ lemon, for garnish

Drizzle of extra virgin olive oil (I like to use garlic-infused olive oil), for garnish

Balsamic glaze, for garnish

Special equipment

Grill pan

TIP

If you don't have a grill pan, you can roast the wraps in a 350°F (180°C) oven for 15 to 20 minutes or until the fruit is soft and tender and the prosciutto is lightly crispy around the edges!

Jessica's Sweet & Salty Salad

SERVES 2–4 | PREP TIME: 10 MINUTES | TOTAL TIME: 20 MINUTES

This is one of my childhood best friend's favorite salads. Jessica would especially crave it when she was pregnant. And although I'm not a doctor (unless you consider me a doctor of love ... but don't do that either because I'm single AF), I don't recommend that anyone who is pregnant eat uncooked cured meats. My way around this is to grill the salty meat-wrapped cheese and sweet fruit before adding it to the salad. It's still one of Jessica's favorites, and now I think it's pretty clear who was really craving this salad!

1. In a large serving bowl, combine the arugula, cucumbers, and walnuts. Set aside.

2. Assemble the prosciutto wraps by laying down a slice of meat, topping it with a slice of peach, and adding a dollop of goat cheese. Fold the prosciutto onto itself to make a little cheese-and-fruit pocket.

3. On a grill or in a grill pan over medium heat, grill the prosciutto wraps for 4 or 5 minutes per side. (Alternatively, you can pan-fry the wraps over medium heat for another 5 minutes or until the prosciutto is crispy and the cheese has begun to melt.) Transfer the wraps to a plate to cool.

4. When the wraps have cooled slightly, add them to the salad. (Leave the wraps whole, or cut them in half to make more yummy bites in the salad.)

5. Garnish the salad with lemon juice, olive oil, and balsamic glaze, and serve. Enjoy!

SOUPER
DUPER SOUPS

Corn Chowder

SERVES 6-8 | PREP TIME: 10 MINUTES | TOTAL TIME: 1 HOUR

The Midwest is known for its corn, and we are corn-loving people—so much so, in fact, that my cousins, who are potato and corn farmers, are known to eat up to eight ears of corn a day during the summer harvest, which I think is wild. I decided to make a soup to showcase corn—the gold you can grow!—inspired by one of my favorite Mexican snacks from when my friends and I road-tripped to Texas to have authentic, kickass barbecue and ribs. This will hold me over until I can make it down south again!

1. In a large pot over medium heat, add the chorizo and cook for 8 to 10 minutes or until completely browned. Transfer to a paper towel–lined plate, and set aside.

2. Add the yellow onion and garlic to the pot, and cook for about 2 minutes. Add the hash browns to soak up all that flavor the chorizo left behind, and cook, stirring occasionally, for about 10 to 15 minutes. Don't let the potatoes stick to the bottom of the pot.

3. Add the butter, if using, cumin, crushed red pepper flakes, smoked paprika, thyme, salt, and pepper. I use about 1 tablespoon of salt to season but not all at once; season in layers.

4. Add the whole-kernel corn,, queso fresco, and queso Oaxaca, and cook, stirring, for 8 to 10 more minutes.

5. When the cheese has melted into everything, slowly pour in the chicken broth while stirring occasionally.

6. Add the creamed corn, and stir to incorporate. Simmer for about 10 to 12 minutes, and add crema. Cook, stirring, for 5 more minutes.

7. Ladle the soup into serving bowls. Garnish with a little more crema, the chorizo, the remaining queso fresco, green onions, cilantro, chili powder, and lime juice, if using, and serve. Enjoy!

1× 9-ounce (255g) package pork chorizo or chorizo of choice

1 yellow onion, roughly chopped

6–8 garlic cloves, minced

3 cups frozen cubed hash browns

3 tablespoons unsalted butter (optional)

2 teaspoons ground cumin

2 teaspoons crushed red pepper flakes

2 teaspoons smoked paprika

1 tablespoon fresh or dried thyme

Salt and freshly ground black pepper

1× 15.25-ounce (432g) can whole-kernel corn or fiesta corn

1× 14.75-ounce (418g) can creamed corn

1× 10-ounce (283g) package queso fresco or cotija, crumbled and divided

½× 10-ounce (283g) package queso Oaxaca, shredded, plus extra for serving

4 cups chicken or vegetable broth

½ cup crema (table cream), plus extra for serving

Sliced green onions, chopped fresh cilantro or parsley, and chili powder, for garnish

1 lime, cut into wedges, for serving (optional, but recommended)

> **········· TIP ·········**
>
> You can chop and boil your own potatoes, but a hack I learned from my mom is to use frozen cubed potatoes. Sometimes they do have salt added, so taste as you go!

2 tablespoons olive oil

2 medium leeks, halved, cleaned of grit, and thinly sliced

2 large carrots, peeled and finely chopped

2 celery stalks, finely chopped

4 garlic cloves, minced

3 cups chopped kale (or more)

2 teaspoons dried oregano

2 tablespoons ground or freshly grated ginger

2 tablespoons mustard powder

1 teaspoon dried or fresh thyme leaves

Salt and freshly ground black pepper

1 cup wild rice, rinsed

4 cups vegetable broth

2 cups butternut squash, peeled and cut into 1-inch (2.5cm) cubes

½ cup cream or coconut cream, plus extra for garnish

1× 15.5-ounce (440g) can chickpeas (garbanzo beans), drained

Chopped fresh chopped parsley, for garnish

TIP

You can add some rotisserie chicken to this recipe if you want to make it a chicken and wild rice soup.

Butternut Squash & Wild Rice Soup

SERVES 4–6 | PREP TIME: 10 MINUTES | TOTAL TIME: 1 HOUR

When you're trying to use up odds and ends in your fridge, soup is a lovely concept. When I developed this recipe, I was shooting for an onion soup with a touch of fall, and whatever else I had in the fridge. It proved to be an excellent dish that many people have craved. It also happens to be vegan (if you use coconut cream in place of the cream). Wild rice is also grown here in some of the great lakes and Canada (along with some other parts of the United States). I highly recommend you check out how wild rice is harvested—it's the coolest process!

1. In a large pot over medium to high heat, add the olive oil, leeks, carrots, celery, and garlic, and sauté for 5 minutes. Add the kale, oregano, ginger, mustard powder, thyme, salt, and pepper. Cover and cook for about 3 to 5 minutes or until the kale has wilted.

2. Add the wild rice, pour in the vegetable broth, and cook for 10 to 15 minutes.

3. Add the butternut squash, and cook for 20 more minutes or until the squash is tender and the rice is cooked.

4. Add the cream along with the chickpeas. Reduce the heat to low, and simmer for about 5 minutes or until heated through.

5. Ladle the soup into serving bowls, garnish with extra cream and parsley, and serve. Enjoy!

6 tablespoons unsalted butter, divided

1 white or yellow onion, finely chopped

2 carrots, finely chopped

2 celery stalks, finely chopped

Salt and freshly ground black pepper

6 garlic cloves, minced

3 tablespoons all-purpose flour

¾ cup light beer

Splash of pickle brine (optional, but highly recommended)

1½ tablespoons stone-ground mustard

1 tablespoon Worcestershire sauce

¼ teaspoon cayenne pepper

1 teaspoon sweet paprika

2 teaspoons Italian seasoning

2½ cups shredded cheddar or a mix of cheeses of choice

4 cups reduced-sodium chicken or vegetable broth

1 cup heavy cream

2 everything bagels, cut into ½-inch (1.25cm) pieces or cubes

Shredded cheese of choice, for garnish

Beer Cheese Soup with Everything Bagel Toasties

SERVES 6-8 | PREP TIME: 15 MINUTES | TOTAL TIME: 35 MINUTES

Being a proud yet honorary cheese head, of course I had to share a Beer Cheese Soup recipe. When I originally shared this recipe online, I noted that it could be eaten alongside my Everything but the Bagel grilled cheese (see Tip) instead of with popcorn. I got so many confused messages because apparently none of my followers have eaten beer cheese with popcorn. I think it must be Midwest thing ... or another reason that I'm an odd meatball. I highly recommend trying it with both!

You can, of course, imagine where I drew my inspiration from— Wisconsin cheese and my grandma's favorite beer, good ol' Budweiser. I'm a fan of their Clydesdale shows and rodeos; we went to a lot when I was a kid. We always loved making this soup at my grandma's house because we never had beer at home when I was growing up, so it was a real treat for all of us. And now hopefully it will be for you, too!

> ·········· **TIP** ··········
>
> Instead of cutting and toasting the bagels, you can make little grilled cheeses with bagels as the bread. I like to make mine with a panini press!

1. In a large pot over medium heat, melt 4 tablespoons of butter. Add the onion, carrots, and celery, and cook for 6-8 minutes or until the vegetables begin to soften and the onion is translucent. Season with salt and pepper, and continue to cook for 8 to 10 more minutes.

2. Add the garlic, and stir for 2 minutes. Add the all-purpose flour, and stir to coat the vegetables. Pour in the light beer, and mix until a slightly creamy/brothy look develops. Add the pickle brine, if using, stone-ground mustard, Worcestershire sauce, cayenne pepper, paprika, and Italian seasoning, and continue to mix.

3. Add the cheddar and chicken broth, and simmer for 10 minutes.

4. Finish with the heavy cream, and stir until combined.

5. While the soup is simmering, add the remaining 2 tablespoons of butter to a large skillet over medium heat. Add the bagel pieces, and toast for about 2 or 3 minutes per side.

6. Ladle the soup into a serving bowl, garnish with toasted bagel pieces (or bagel grilled cheese! (see Tip) and cheese, and serve. Enjoy!

Sheet Pan Tomato Soup

SERVES 6-8 | PREP TIME: 10 MINUTES | TOTAL TIME: 1 HOUR

I could happily eat a bowl of soup every day, regardless of the weather. I also like to think of soup merely as a suggestive dip if you have a sandwich nearby. But then I end up eating like 10 sandwiches a day. Soup is great for sharing, and to me it feels very cozy, which is the feeling I want people to have when they walk into my house. I especially love this soup because it's so easy to make, and it doesn't need to sit on the stove forever. Tomato soup is a sure bet for kids. Sometimes I like to add alphabet pasta to mine when I'm feeling nostalgic.

1. Preheat the oven to 350°F (180°C).

2. In a 9×13 (23×33cm) casserole dish, add the tomatoes, red onion, carrots, and garlic. Add the salt and pepper to taste. Top with the extra virgin olive oil, bay leaf, crushed red pepper flakes, smoked paprika, and cumin.

3. Roast for 30 to 45 minutes or the vegetables are soft and tender.

4. Remove from the oven. Discard the bay leaf. Gently squeeze the roasted garlic into a blender along with half of the dill. (If you're feeling lazy and don't want to chop the dill, DON'T! It's getting blended anyways.) Add the remaining contents of the roasting dish and the vegetable broth, and blend high or purée, depending on your blender, for about 5 minutes or a few minutes longer until it's the type of creamy you like your soup!

5. Pour the soup into the serving bowls. Top with heavy cream, extra virgin olive oil, and more fresh dill if you like. Add a drizzle of honey over the top (it's a real game changer!), and serve. Enjoy!

8 large tomatoes

1 red onion, roughly chopped

2 carrots, roughly chopped

2 heads of garlic, unpeeled, tops cut off

½ tablespoon salt

Freshly ground black pepper

¼ cup extra virgin olive oil, plus extra for garnish

1 bay leaf

1 tablespoon crushed red pepper flakes (reduce if sensitive to heat)

1 tablespoon smoked paprika

½ tablespoon ground cumin

1 bunch fresh dill, chopped and divided, plus extra for garnish

4 cups vegetable broth, chicken broth, or broth of choice

1 cup heavy cream or coconut milk

Honey, for garnish

Special equipment
Blender

Roasted Red Pepper Soup

SERVES 6-8 | PREP TIME: 10 MINUTES | TOTAL TIME: 1 HOUR

2 white or yellow onions, roughly chopped

2 carrots, roughly chopped

3-4 bell red peppers, ribs and seeds removed

1 pint (10 ounces/285g) cherry tomatoes

1× 15-ounce (425g) can butter beans or cannellini beans

1 head of garlic

Salt and freshly ground black pepper (I use about ½ tablespoon salt)

½ teaspoon cayenne pepper (optional)

1 tablespoon dried oregano

1 tablespoon sweet paprika

2 bay leaves

Small bunch fresh thyme, plus extra for garnish

A few sprigs of fresh rosemary

½ cup extra-virgin olive oil, plus extra for garnish

4 cups chicken or vegetable broth

Heavy cream or coconut milk, Parmesan, crushed red pepper flakes, chopped fresh chives, for garnish (optional)

Special equipment

Blender

In this recipe, I'll show you an easy way to make soups creamier without adding cream (even though I list it as an optional garnish). Beans are creamy, and when blended, they can turn other things creamy, too. This soup is easy to turn into a 10/10 vegan (using vegetable broth instead of chicken) recipe that, quite frankly, everyone enjoys. And if it's humanly possible to be sick of soup, you can turn this into a romesco!

I recommend grabbing some sort of carb for dipping—a crusty bread that's not too hard, perhaps, or something with air to catch all the soup.

1. Preheat the oven to 350°F (180°C).

2. In a large casserole dish or shallow roasting pan, combine the onions, carrots, red peppers, cherry tomatoes, butter beans, garlic, salt, black pepper, cayenne pepper, if using, oregano, paprika, bay leaves, thyme, and rosemary. Add the olive oil, and toss to coat well.

3. Bake for 45 minutes. You want to start to see char developing just around the edges of the peppers.

4. Remove from the oven, and let it sit for 5 minutes.

5. Remove and discard the rosemary, thyme, and bay leaves. Add the rest of the contents of the casserole dish to a heat-safe blender and then pour in the juices, too. Add the chicken broth to the blender, and blend on high for about 3 to 5 minutes or until it's smooth and creamy. Taste to see if it needs more salt and black pepper.

6. Pour the soup into serving bowls. Garnish with whatever feels right—I like to use a ton of Parmesan, crushed red pepper flakes, and whatever fresh herbs I have in my garden or fridge—and serve. Enjoy!

Blender Lobster Bisque

SERVES 3-4 | PREP TIME: 5 MINUTES | TOTAL TIME: 1 HOUR

It may not be obvious or apparent to everyone, but I don't tend to do things the "traditional way." I have no doubt in my mind that a lot of people who went to school for professional culinary training might stick up their nose at some of my ideas. That's okay, and I love that for them! However, I'm more concerned with sharing approachable recipes and getting people in the kitchen to enjoy the cooking process—and doing it in a way that everyone, from every walk of life, can love.

This rich, decadent, and seemingly challenging soup is made with one pan and one blender. Originally, I wanted to make this for the man of my dreams—who still hasn't appeared quite yet—so I'll make it for you instead. Any soup that qualifies as a "bisque" is going to be party time in your mouth. Serve with crusty bread and a nice, crisp white wine.

2 yellow onions, halved

2 carrots, peeled and roughly chopped

2 celery stalks, roughly chopped

2 pints (20 ounces/560g) cherry or Roma tomatoes

2 shallots, halved

1 head of garlic, unpeeled, top cut off

½ cup olive oil, plus extra for garnish

1 lemon, halved

Salt and freshly ground black pepper

2 teaspoons dried rosemary

2 teaspoons dried basil

2 teaspoons sweet paprika

2 teaspoons fresh or dried parsley

8 tablespoons unsalted butter

4-6 lobster tails, thawed if frozen, shell cut, meat on top (about 8-16 ounces/225-450g total)

4 cups fish or vegetable broth

½ cup heavy cream, plus extra for garnish

Torn fresh basil and chopped fresh chives, for garnish

Serve with

Crusty bread

Special equipment

Blender

1. Preheat the oven to 400°F (200°C).

2. In a 9×13-inch (23×33cm) casserole dish or shallow roasting pan, add the yellow onions, carrots, celery, cherry tomatoes, shallots, garlic, olive oil, lemon half, salt, pepper, rosemary, basil, paprika, and parsley. Toss to coat everything in the oil, and bake for 35 to 40 minutes. You're welcome for the amazing smells about to come out of your kitchen.

3. Remove from the oven. Top with the lobster, cover the lobster tails with the butter, and mix. Return to the oven, and bake for 15 to 20 more minutes.

4. When the lobster is fully cooked, you can remove it from the shell, and discard the shell or keep it as is for presentation, I recommend using half of the meat to put into the soup.

5. Add half of the meat, any leftover juice from the lemon rind to a blender, and squeeze in the garlic along with the roasted vegetables. Add the fish broth and the heavy cream, and purée for about 5 minutes (or less, depending on your blender) or until smooth and creamy.

6. Pour the soup into a bowl, and add any of the "presentation" lobster meat or keep it on the side to eat with your soup. Garnish with more heavy cream, basil, and chives, and serve with some crusty bread. Enjoy!

······························ **TIPS** ······························

Carefully cut the lobster tails open using kitchen scissors and place the meat on top, trying to keep the meat in one piece. (I recommend watching a quick YouTube tutorial!)

I'm going to teach you a food styling tip that is so easy but looks super fancy: For a cool design on top of your soup, pour a couple drops of heavy cream onto the soup, grab a skewer, and run the skewer in a circular motion through the cream, ending in the middle of the circle. Then garnish with a bit of fresh herbs on top, and serve.

Pickle Soup

SERVES 6 | PREP TIME: 10 MINUTES | TOTAL TIME: 45 MINUTES

3 russet potatoes (about 2–3 pounds/
1–1.5kg), peeled and diced, or 3 cups
diced frozen potatoes

3 tablespoons extra virgin olive oil

1 yellow onion, diced

2 celery stalks, roughly chopped

2 carrots, peeled and roughly chopped

6 garlic cloves, minced

Salt and freshly ground black pepper

2 tablespoons unsalted butter

4 tablespoons all-purpose flour

4 cups vegetable or chicken broth

1 heaping cup chopped dill pickles
(about 5–6 pickles)

½ cup pickle brine

1 bunch fresh dill, divided, plus extra for
garnish

2 bay leaves

1 teaspoon fresh thyme, stems removed

1 cup freshly grated Havarti

½ cup heavy cream, plus extra for
garnish

Sriracha, for garnish

This is my world-famous, not-very-traditional Zupa Ogórkowa (aka pickle soup). I did not name it that; the wonderful people of the internet did. This soup was introduced to us when my very Polish great-grandma came to live with my family. Before I first wrapped my chompers around this hearty, tangy, PICKLEY soup, I had my doubts, but after that first taste, I knew immediately that I loved it forever and always. BFFs forever. Pinkie swear realness. 4ever.

If there's one recipe I will always be known for, it could be this one. And it makes sense because this soup is bomb as hell. I initially posted it to share with all the pickle lovers, and the number of people who have reached out to tell me that they triple the recipe because they go through it so quickly is astonishing. I hope you enjoy it also! Pickle people unite!

TIPS

If you'd like an addition, I grew up eating this with garlic bread.

My family and I love to play "bay leaf bingo" with soup, sooo, if you get a bay leaf in your bowl of soup you win a bingo and good luck, and another serving of soup! B-i-n-g-t-f-o because its the best, and so are you! Discard the bay leaf and enjoy!

1. In a large pot over high heat, bring 6 cups of salted water to a boil. Add the russet potatoes, and cook for 20 minutes. Drain the potatoes, and set aside in the colander.

2. In the same pot over medium heat, add the extra virgin olive oil, yellow onion, celery, carrots, and garlic, and cook for about 8 to 10 minutes or until the onion is translucent. Season with salt and pepper. (I use about 1 teaspoon each.)

3. Add the butter to the pan and melt. Add the all-purpose flour, and mix until coated.

4. Slowly incorporate the vegetable broth in batches while stirring, not all at once. You'll see the soup change to a light, creamy color.

5. Add the potatoes, dill pickles, pickle brine, dill, bay leaves, and thyme, and simmer for 20 to 30 minutes.

6. Add the Havarti and heavy cream, and mix well. Remove and discard the bay leaves.

7. Ladle the soup onto serving bowls. Add a drizzle of heavy cream, sriracha, and fresh dill for garnish, and serve. Enjoy!

Chicken Tortilla Soup

SERVES 6–8 | PREP TIME: 10 MINUTES | TOTAL TIME: 35 MINUTES

I genuinely love soup. It's filling, it makes me feel better, and it feels like home. It also can be used to stretch a meal for a longer time, and it's a great way to bring new life to leftovers! Chicken Tortilla Soup is always on the menu anytime I have extra ingredients left over from Taco Tuesday. You can apply this concept to whatever leftovers you have on hand and soupify the contents of your fridge!

1. In a large pot over medium to high heat, heat the olive oil for about 1 minute. Add the chicken, and cook for about 4 or 5 minutes per side, season with paprika and oregano on each side with salt and pepper as you cook, until the internal temperature reaches 165°F (75°C).

2. Transfer the chicken to a plate, and shred or cut into bite-size pieces.

3. Add the butter to the pot to melt. Add the onion, celery, carrots, and garlic, and season with salt and pepper. Cook for about 8 to 10 minutes or until the vegetables begin to soften and the onion is translucent.

4. Add the black beans, corn, and chipotles in adobo, and stir to combine. Slowly incorporate the chicken broth. Bring to a simmer, return the chicken to the pot, and cook, stirring occasionally, for 10 minutes.

5. Ladle the soup into serving bowls. Garnish with avocado, jalapeño, cotija, tortilla strips, a little dollop of sour cream, cilantro, or green onion, if using, and serve. Enjoy!

3 tablespoons olive oil or avocado oil

3–4 boneless chicken breasts (about 1½–2 pounds/680g–1kg)

Salt and freshly ground black pepper

2 teaspoons ground cumin

2 teaspoons paprika

2 teaspoons fresh or dried oregano

4 tablespoons unsalted butter

1 white or yellow onion, chopped

2 celery stalks, chopped

2 carrots, peeled and chopped

5–6 garlic cloves, minced

1× 15-ounce (456g) can black beans, drained and rinsed

1× 15-ounce (456g) can corn, drained

½× 7-ounce (100g) can chipotles in adobo

4 cups chicken broth

Chopped avocado, sliced jalapeño, cotija, tortilla strips, sour cream, fresh cilantro, and sliced green onion, for garnish (optional)

Special equipment

Meat thermometer

> ·········· **TIP** ··········
>
> If you can't find tortilla strips, you can make them yourself by cutting a tortilla into strips and frying them in oil. Or just use tortilla chips!

Knophela (Little German Button Soup)

SERVES 6-8 | PREP TIME: 20 MINUTES | TOTAL TIME: 45 MINUTES

In some circles, this soup is considered the North Dakota state dish, but it's relatively unknown outside the area. I hope you realize that sharing this recipe is like me sharing one of my favorite indie bands that I love and want to keep to myself because you know everyone else is going to love them and be obsessed with them and if they become mainstream it's going to be "less cool." But it's good to share and grow and give everyone their time in the spotlight, so it's officially time to share this soup with you.

Although it's a dish that's not very well known, when people try it, it becomes their new favorite. It's called "button soup" because the dumplings are in the shape of tiny, tasty little buttons. You get dumplings in every single bite...I don't think I have to say more. That should sell the soup itself. It's pronounced "nef-la," by the way, for when you're walking around, declaring to the world that it's your newfound favorite soup, because you're as cute as a button, like this soup. Also, it can be made vegan if you prefer.

I've had quite a few grandmothers' versions of this soup, and I know this recipe is not totally traditional. But but I wanted to do my best to expedite the process to get it into your belly faster! I have never ever seen anyone add any lick of spice to this soup, and I'm changing that because it's simply better.

3 tablespoons olive oil

8 tablespoons unsalted butter

1 white or yellow onion, finely chopped

2 carrots, peeled and finely chopped

2 celery stalks, finely chopped

2 russet potatoes, peeled and roughly chopped (about 3-4 cups), or cubed frozen hash browns

5-6 garlic cloves, minced

4 tablespoons all-purpose flour

1 tablespoon poultry seasoning or bouillon cube

1 tablespoon Italian seasoning

1 tablespoon fresh or dried dill, plus extra for garnish

1½ teaspoons crushed red pepper flakes

1 teaspoon dried oregano

Heavy pinch of nutmeg

2 bay leaves

4 cups chicken broth or vegetable broth

1 cup heavy cream or milk of choice

2 pounds (1kg) store-bought gnocchi or homemade dumplings (see page 206)

Chopped fresh parsley, for garnish

1. In a large pot over medium heat, add the butter, onion, carrot, celery, russet potatoes, and garlic, and cook for about 8 to 10 minutes or until the onion is translucent.

2. Add the all-purpose flour to coat, followed by the poultry seasoning, Italian seasoning, dill, crushed red pepper flakes, oregano, nutmeg, and bay leaves. Slowly add the chicken broth and heavy cream, and stir. Bring to a light boil or summer, stirring occasionally.

3. If you're using homemade dumpling dough, flour your work surface, and roll the dough into a long log about ¼ inch (6mm) thick. Cut it into small cubes. Toss them in a little extra flour if needed so they don't stick to each other.

4. Add the gnocchi or dumplings to the boiling soup, and cook for about 10 to 15 minutes or until they float.

5. Ladle the soup into serving bowls, garnish with parsley, and serve with something good for dipping. Enjoy!

> .... **TIP** ....
>
> If you're pinched for time and don't feel like making your own dumplings (which I totally get), you can use premade gnocchi. But the dumplings are one of my favorite parts of this recipe.

Chicken & Dumpling Soup

SERVES 6-8 | PREP TIME: 10 MINUTES | TOTAL TIME: 45 MINUTES

This is a family favorite that I zhuzhed up a little. When I was little it was known as "Feel Better Soup" because it's so cozy, and with the massive dumplings, it feels similar to matzo ball soup. It doesn't always make you feel better if you're suffering from some sort of illness other than a cold, and I don't know that it's necessarily good to eat too much dairy if you're sick, but no matter how stuffed up or congested you might be, you can always taste it! It's a rich soup with tons of fresh herbs and flavor—like a roast chicken but in soup form! It's best eaten for any and all occasions, but it's especially good on fall or winter days when you need some warming up! If you are new here and you haven't already made this, you are going to lu–uh–uh–uh–ovve it.

3–4 tablespoons olive oil

3–4 boneless, skinless chicken breasts (about 1½-2 pounds/450-900g), sprinkled with salt and freshly ground black pepper

1 teaspoon poultry seasoning

1 teaspoon ground ginger

1 teaspoon tarragon or Italian seasoning

1 teaspoon ground cumin

2 carrots, shredded or cut into matchsticks

1 yellow onion, roughly chopped

2 celery stalks, roughly chopped

3–4 garlic cloves, minced

4 tablespoons unsalted butter

4 tablespoons all-purpose flour

6 cups chicken broth

½ cup heavy whipping cream or buttermilk

2 sprigs of rosemary

2 bay leaves

Chopped fresh dill and parsley, and crushed red pepper flakes, for garnish

For the dumplings

2 cups all-purpose flour

1 tablespoon baking powder

Salt and freshly ground black pepper

1½ cups heavy cream or buttermilk

1. In a large soup pot over medium-high heat, add the olive oil and chicken. Add the poultry seasoning, ground ginger, tarragon, and cumin on top of the chicken, and sear on both sides for 8 to 10 minutes or until a slightly brown crust develops.

2. Cook for 5 to 7 more minutes per side, and then remove the chicken from the pot. Cut or shred the chicken to your desired texture, and set aside.

3. Add the carrots, yellow onion, and celery to the pot, and cook for 10 minutes or until the onion is translucent. Add the garlic and butter, and return the shredded chicken to the pot. Sprinkle the all-purpose flour on top to coat everything and then slowly stir in the chicken broth until a smooth texture develops. Stir in the heavy cream, add the rosemary and bay leaves, and simmer for about 10 minutes.

4. Meanwhile, make the dumplings. In a medium bowl, whisk together the flour, baking powder, salt, and pepper. Add the heavy cream, and use a rubber spatula to work the mixture into a dough.

5. Using your hands, form the dough into balls about the size of the circle created by touching the tip of your index finger to the tip of your thumb. Or use an ice cream scoop. You can make the dumplings bigger, but allow more cook time and possibly more broth if so. Add the dumplings to the simmering broth, cover, and cook for 10 to 15 minutes or until they've doubled in size. Remove and discard the bay leaves.

6. Ladle the soup into bowls. Garnish with dill, parsley, and crushed red pepper flakes, and serve. Enjoy!

YOU WANNA PIZZA ME?

Margarita Pizza with Homemade Pizza Dough

MARGARITA PIZZA SERVES 4-6 | PREP TIME: 10 MINUTES | TOTAL TIME: 45 MINUTES
HOMEMADE DOUGH MAKES 1 LARGE (12-INCH [30.5CM]) OR 2 MEDIUM (6-INCH [15CM]) PIZZA CRUSTS
PREP TIME: 1 HOUR | TOTAL TIME: 1 HOUR 35 MINUTES

Margarita pizza is traditionally a Neapolitan-style pie with an emphasis on San Marzano tomatoes. I love it for its fresh flavors, featuring two of my favorite ingredients, tomatoes and basil (which, along with the white mozzarella, are meant to represent the Italian flag). I consider this a summer recipe simply because that's when our tomatoes are at their best!

Usually, this type of pizza is cooked in a pizza oven at a very high temperature to achieve its incredible chewy and charred smoky crust flavor. I don't have an especially high-powered oven, but I do have a skillet and a grill or campfire! It's not quite the same as how they do it in Naples, and I'm not trying to sell it to you like it is, but it's the closest I've come without having owned a pizza oven. But don't worry, I also have a method that will work in your home oven all year round.

It's kind of important to nail the timing, so follow the steps closely for best results.

Oven Method

1. Preheat the oven to 400°F (200°C).

2. In a 12-inch (30.5cm) cast-iron or oven-safe skillet, add 2 tablespoons of olive oil and rotate the pan so the entire skillet is oiled. Pop the skillet into the oven to warm while you prep the rest of the ingredients.

3. Using a rolling pin, roll out the Homemade Pizza Dough on a floured surface into a circular shape, shoot for about 12-inch (30.5cm) diameter (to fit the skillet).

4. Remove the skillet from the oven, place the dough in the skillet, and brush the remaining 2 tablespoons of olive oil over the top. Bake for 10 minutes.

5. In a small bowl, add the tomatoes. (Crush the tomatoes gently with your hands if you're using canned.) Season with salt and pepper, add garlic and Italian seasoning, and mix to combine.

6. Remove the skillet from the oven and flip over the dough. Spread the tomato sauce evenly over the crust, and distribute the burrata and provolone over the sauce. Bake for 15 to 20 minutes or until you start to see all the melty goodness on top.

7. Be sure you have some heavy-duty oven mitts on, and remove the pan from the oven. Let it cool for a few minutes because that mf'er is going to be HOT. Drizzle a little olive oil over the top of the pizza, and sprinkle with fresh basil and crushed red pepper flakes. Cut into slices, and serve. Enjoy!

4 tablespoons olive oil, divided, plus more for drizzling

1 pound (450g) Homemade Pizza Dough (recipe to follow)

1 pint (10 ounces/285g) cherry tomatoes or San Marzano tomatoes, sliced, or 14 ounces (400g) canned whole tomatoes, drained

Salt and freshly ground black pepper

4–6 garlic cloves, minced

1 tablespoon Italian seasoning

8 ounces (225g) burrata or fresh mozzarella, torn

1 cup freshly grated provolone or Parmesan

Handful of fresh basil

Pinch crushed red pepper flakes (optional, but recommended)

Special equipment
Rolling pin

Campfire method

1. Heat the embers until very hot or until they're smoldering with no flame and arrange a grate over the top.

2. Follow steps 2 through 4 of the oven method. Depending on how hot your fire is, cook for 5 to 10 minutes or until the crust is starting to brown.

3. Pull the skillet off the fire—it will be hot so be sure you're using mitts. Flip over the dough, and add the sauce and cheeses. Cover the skillet with a lid or foil, and put it back over the fire. You'll smell when it's cooking, but only check it after 10 to 15 minutes, when you think it might be done. Remove from the heat, garnish as directed, and serve.

> ·········· **TIPS** ··········
>
> Pat dry the burrata (or mozzarella, if using) before placing it on the pizza to remove any excess moisture and whey.
>
> If you're cooking your pizza over the campfire, be sure you have a lid or some foil to cover the skillet.

Homemade Pizza Dough

1. In the bowl of a stand mixer fitted with the dough hook, mix the flour, sugar, Italian seasoning, salt, yeast, and warm water on medium for 5 to 8 minutes. Or add the ingredients to a large bowl and stir by hand using a rubber spatula until the dough comes together and is slightly sticky.

2. Transfer the dough to glass or plastic bowl or container that's been lightly coated with oil. Let the dough rise in a warm spot for 1 hour (I usually plop the bowl on a warm stovetop with the burners off).

3. When the dough has doubled in size, turn it out onto a floured surface. The dough should be pliable at this stage so you can roll it out by hand or with the rolling pin to your desired shape.

For the Homemade Pizza Dough

2½ cups all-purpose flour

1 tablespoon granulated sugar

2 teaspoons Italian seasoning

Salt

1 packet instant yeast

1 cup warm water

Olive oil, for coating

Special equipment

Stand mixer with a dough hook

Rolling pin

Supreme Sheet Pan Pizza
with Homemade Ranch Dressing

SUPREME PIZZA SERVES 4–6 | PREP TIME: 45 MINUTES | TOTAL TIME:45 MINUTES
HOMEMADE RANCH SERVES 4–6 | PREP TIME: 45 MINUTES | TOTAL TIME:45 MINUTES

I don't just like pizza. I LIKE, like pizza…like, a LOT. And like a lot of other people, I'm sure, I could eat pizza every day if it was humanly possible and socially acceptable. When I think of sheet pan pizza, I'm reminded of how pizza was served in my elementary and high schools. This is in a much different category but brain food nonetheless!

Supreme pizza is great because it has a little bit of protein and a little bit of veggies— it's basically a balanced meal. My dad is the reason I load up all my pizzas with so many toppings. He's the king of supreme pizzas. He's an "everything" guy and loves the combination of all the meats and cheeses. I think you'll love it, too. Don't forget the ranch!

3 ounces (85g) bacon, sliced

3 ounces (85g) sausage, crumbled or cut into bite size pieces

½ white or yellow onion, thinly sliced

4-5 garlic cloves, minced

4-5 portobello mushrooms, thinly sliced

½ green bell pepper, ribs and seeds removed and sliced or roughly chopped

Sprinkle of all-purpose flour, for dusting

1 pound (450g) Homemade Pizza Dough (see page 210) or store-bought pizza dough

½ cup spicy marinara sauce or arrabbiata sauce

8 ounces (225g) fresh mozzarella, shredded, or whatever you have on hand

3 ounces (85g) pepperoni, sliced

Handful of mixed pitted black and green olives, sliced (optional)

Grated Parmesan, crushed red pepper flakes, and hot sauce, for garnish

Homemade Ranch Dressing (recipe to follow), for dipping

Special equipment

Rolling pin

1. Preheat the oven to 350°F (180°C).

2. In a medium pan over medium heat, cook the bacon and sausage for 8 to 10 minutes or until browned. Transfer to a paper towel–lined plate to drain.

3. Add the onion, garlic, portobello mushrooms, and green pepper to the pan, and sauté for 6 to 8 minutes or until everything is either glossy or has some color, then transfer the veggies to a clean plate.

4. Lightly flour your work surface, and use a rolling pin to roll out the dough to fit the baking sheet you're using. Gently transfer the dough to the baking sheet.

5. Spread the marinara sauce in an even layer over the dough, leaving a ½- to 1 inch (1.25–2.5cm) border around the edges. Top with mozzarella and then add the pepperoni, bacon, sausage, vegetables, and olives.

6. Bake for 25 to 30 minutes or until the crust has started to turn golden.

7. Remove from the oven and let cool for a few minutes on the baking sheet. Garnish with Parmesan, crushed red pepper flakes, and hot sauce; cut into slices; and serve with a side of ranch for dipping. Enjoy!

Homemade Ranch Dressing

In a medium bowl, whisk together all the ingredients, adapting the ratios and ingredients as you like.

2 teaspoons chopped fresh chives

2 teaspoons fresh parsley

2 teaspoons dried dill

2 tablespoons onion powder

2 tablespoons garlic powder

½ teaspoon cayenne pepper

½ cup mayonnaise, Greek yogurt, or sour cream

¼ cup whole milk or buttermilk

Splash of pickle juice

> ······················· **TIPS** ·······················
>
> I like to make my ranch dressing with a little Greek yogurt to sneak some probiotics into my diet without even thinking about it. If you want it to be like the ranch dressing you get in a restaurant, I recommend using mayo.
>
> Let the mixture get to know itself in the fridge for at least half an hour. The flavor will really build!
>
> I like to keep a batch of the dry seasonings used in this recipe on hand so I can throw together fresh dressing or dip at a moment's notice.

Sprinkle of all-purpose flour, for dusting

1 pound (450g) Homemade Pizza Dough (see page 210) or store-bought pizza dough

1 tablespoon olive oil

4 garlic cloves, minced

5–8 ounces (140–225g) fresh mozzarella, sliced or torn

1 teaspoon dried oregano

1 teaspoon crushed red pepper flakes

1 cup homemade or store-bought marinara sauce

1 cup homemade or store-bought vodka sauce

1 cup Delishaas Pesto (see page 127) or store-bought pesto

½ cup grated Parmesan

Special equipment

Rolling pin

TIPS

You can add any toppings to this pizza, but it's all about the sauce, baby!

This is a friendly reminder that you're amazing and beautiful. Also, be sure to keep in mind that if you're making the dough from scratch, you're adding another hour to this recipe because the dough needs time to rise.

The MVP
(Marinara, Vodka Cream, & Pesto)

SERVES 4–6 | PREP TIME: 10 MINUTES | TOTAL TIME: 45 MINUTES

Hot take: I like eating pizza for the cheese and the sauce. If the crust isn't up to my standards, it can be remedied with some good sauce to dip it in or I love sharing it with my dog. This pizza is called the MVP not only because it's the most valuable player in the pizza game, but also because it stands for my favorite things: marinara, vodka, and pesto—the saucy trinity. This may not be everyone's MVP, but it sure as hell is mine.

1. Preheat the oven to 350°F (180°C).

2. Lightly flour your work surface, and use a rolling pin to roll out the dough to fit the baking sheet you're using. Gently transfer the dough to the baking sheet.

3. Drizzle olive oil over the dough, starting in the center and working outward, leaving a ½- to 1 inch (1.25–2.5cm) border around the edges. Distribute the minced garlic in the same manner and spread into an even layer over the oil. Then top with mozzarella, oregano, and crushed red pepper flakes.

4. Bake for 12 to 15 minutes or until the dough is about halfway cooked.

5. Remove from the oven, and add the marinara and vodka sauces and pesto over the cheese in any pattern you'd like. Lines work best to ensure you get little in each bite. Top the sauces with the Parmesan.

6. Bake for 12 to 15 more minutes or until the crust has started to turn golden.

7. Remove from the oven and let cool for a few minutes on the baking sheet. Cut into slices and serve. Enjoy!

Salad Pizza

SERVES 4-6 | PREP TIME: 10 MINUTES | TOTAL TIME: 45 MINUTES

Okay, okay ... this didn't quite make the cut for the salad chapter because it is NOT a salad. But there are enough vegetables and other green things on this pizza to make you feel like you're eating a salad. (Lovers of olives and pickled things, head to the front of the line!) This is something I make on weeknights when it's not Pizza Friday (or Pizza Saturday) and I can't justify eating an entire meaty pie. Feel free to totally rip off Pizza Bagels theme song and sing, "Pizza in the morning, pizza in the evening, pizza at supper time! When you've got salad on a pizza, you can eat pizza any time!" as you make and eat it.

1. Preheat the oven to 350°F (180°C).

2. Lightly flour your work surface, and use a rolling pin to roll out the dough to fit the baking sheet you're using. Gently transfer the dough to the baking sheet.

3. Evenly spread the Delishaas Pesto evenly over the dough, leaving a ½- to 1 inch (1.25–2.5cm) border around the edges. Evenly distribute the sun-dried tomatoes, onion, roasted peppers, and Kalamata olives over the pesto.

4. In a small bowl, toss together the oregano, Parmesan, fontina, goat cheese, arugula, spinach, and giardiniera so it all sort of sticks together. Add to the top of the pizza in an even layer.

5. Bake for 25 to 30 minutes or until the crust has started to turn golden.

6. Remove from the oven and let cool for a few minutes on the baking sheet. Garnish with crushed red pepper flakes or your desired toppings, cut into slices, and serve. Enjoy!

Sprinkle of all-purpose flour, for dusting

1 pound (450g) Homemade Pizza Dough (see page 210) or store-bought pizza dough

½ cup Delishaas Pesto (see page 127) or store-bought pesto

½ cup sun-dried tomatoes

1 white or yellow onion, cut into thin slices

3–4 roasted peppers, roughly chopped

¼ cup Kalamata olives, pitted and roughly chopped (optional)

Few sprigs of oregano, roughly chopped

½ cup shaved or grated Parmesan, plus extra for garnish

½ cup shaved or grated fontina

4 ounces (115g) goat cheese, crumbled

1 cup arugula

1 cup spinach, chopped

½ cup giardiniera, drained (I recommend mild)

Crushed red pepper flakes, for garnish

Special equipment

Rolling pin

> **TIP**
>
> If you aren't a big fan of pesto, that's totally fine. I've been known to use hummus instead of pesto for this recipe when I don't have the urge to do anything else or don't feel like running to the store; your favorite hummus will probably pair famously with all of this veg!

Tomato Feta Lavash

SERVES 3-4 | PREP TIME: 30 MINUTES | TOTAL TIME: 1 HOUR

5 ½ ounces (150g) feta or Boursin (any flavor)

¼ cup olive oil

1 head of garlic, top removed

2 pints (20 ounces/560g) cherry tomatoes

1 large lavash cracker crust (about 16 ounces/450g)

8 ounces (225g) fresh mozzarella, torn or sliced

Crushed red pepper flakes, grated Parmesan, handful of fresh basil, for garnish

Technically, I'm a TikToker, in the sense that as a creator, TikTok is my largest platform currently. It never fails that people are surprised that I make a living sharing content for free. When I take the time to explain my career to people, it tends to broaden their perspective, or at least I like to pretend it does.

This creation is an ode to a recipe originally posted on the Finnish food blog Liemessä by Jenni Häyrinen, which came to be known as THE TikTok pasta. It was so simple and easy to prepare that it took the world by storm. The flavor profile of this recipe is similar, but I've piled the toppings on a flatbread crust and turned it into a pizza situation. Everybody's so creative!

1. Preheat the oven to 350°F (180°C).

2. In a medium baking dish, combine the feta, olive oil, garlic, and cherry tomatoes. Bake for 30 minutes or until the tomatoes and garlic are soft.

3. Place the lavash crust on a baking sheet. Spread the contents of the baking dish on top of the lavash leaving a ½- to 1-inch (1.25–2.5cm) border around the edges, and then top with mozzarella. Bake on the top oven rack for 10 minutes or until the cheese has melted.

4. Remove from the oven and let cool for a few minutes on the baking sheet. Garnish with crushed red pepper flakes, Parmesan, and basil; cut into slices; and serve. Enjoy!

Pickle Pizza

SERVES 4-6 | PREP TIME: 10 MINUTES | TOTAL TIME: 45 MINUTES

I want you to think back to when you were a kid. You probably began eating cheese pizza with no other toppings. (There's no shame in that. It's still a bop.) As you began to grow up, your taste buds developed and you likely added pepperoni pizza to the mix, then meat lovers, then supreme—or at least that's how it was growing up in my house. I invite you to level up one step further and try this delectable pickle pizza. You don't even have to be a pickle stan like I am.

1. Preheat the oven to 350°F (180°C).

2. Lightly flour your work surface, and use a rolling pin to roll out the dough to fit the baking sheet you're using. Gently transfer the dough to the baking sheet.

3. Drizzle the garlic-infused olive oil over the dough, starting in the center and working outward, leaving a ½- to 1-inch (1.25–2.5cm) border around the edges. Distribute the minced garlic in the same manner and spread into an even layer over the oil. Top with the dill Havarti, pepperoni, dill pickles, and Parmesan.

4. Bake for 25 to 30 minutes or until the crust has started to turn golden. Start checking for doneness after 20 minutes. It's going to smell amazing!

5. Remove from the oven and let cool for a few minutes on the baking sheet. Garnish with crushed red pepper flakes, if using, and fresh dill; drizzle with sriracha and Homemade Ranch Dressing; cut into slices; and serve. Enjoy!

Sprinkle of all-purpose flour, for dusting

1 pound (450g) Homemade Pizza Dough (see page 210) or store-bought pizza dough

¼ cup garlic-infused olive oil, or plain olive oil

4-5 garlic cloves, minced

8 ounces (225g) dill Havarti (or regular Havarti if you can't find dill), grated

4 ounces (115g) pepperoni or ham, roughly chopped

6-8 ounces dill pickle chips or slices, dried with a paper towel

2 ounces (55g) freshly grated Parmesan

1 teaspoon crushed red pepper flakes, for garnish (optional)

½ bunch fresh dill, for garnish

Sriracha and Homemade Ranch Dressing (see page 212), for drizzling

Special equipment

Rolling pin

TIPS

Be sure to dry the pickle slices with a paper towel before adding them to the pizza. The juice is the enemy on this pie.

More cheese is always going to please me, especially on this pizza!

Sprinkle of all-purpose flour, for dusting

1 pound (450g) Homemade Pizza Dough (see page 210), store-bought pizza dough, or naan

2 cups homemade or store-bought marinara sauce

½ teaspoon ground ginger

½ teaspoon ground cumin

½ teaspoon harissa powder (if you like spice; if not, use ½ teaspoon smoked paprika)

4 tablespoons Delishaas Pesto (see page 127) or store-bought pesto, plus extra for garnish

16 ounces (450g) burrata, torn, grated mozzarella, or crumbled feta

½ red onion, sliced

4-6 garlic cloves, minced

1 pint (10 ounces/285g) cherry tomatoes, sliced in half

3 ounces (85g) prosciutto, thinly sliced (optional)

5-6 large eggs

½ bunch fresh cilantro or parsley, chopped

Special equipment

Rolling pin

Shakshuka Pizza

SERVES 3-4 | PREP TIME: 10 MINUTES | TOTAL TIME: 45 MINUTES

After giving myself permission to indulge in my fantasy of trying a runny fried egg on pizza with my Gas Station Breakfast Pizza (see page 32), and noting my love of runny eggs in shakshuka, I realized that I could bring these dishes together by utilizing some leftover brunch shakshuka. Shakshuka pizza—it makes perfect sense! Another excuse to make pizza for breakfast!

1. Preheat the oven to 350°F (180°C).

2. Lightly flour your work surface, and use a rolling pin to roll out the dough to fit the baking sheet you're using. Gently transfer the dough to the baking sheet. (If you're using naan, place it on the baking sheet.)

3. In a medium bowl, combine the marinara sauce, ginger, cumin, and harissa powder, if using. Spread the sauce over the pizza dough, leaving a ½- to 1-inch (1.25–2.5cm) border around the edges. Liberally add the pesto in small dollops, or mix it into the sauce—either works! If using burrata, crack that open and spread it everywhere; otherwise, sprinkle the grated mozzarella or crumbled feta. Top the cheese with the red onion, garlic, cherry tomatoes, and prosciutto, if using.

4. One at a time, crack the eggs over the other toppings. Try to crack them toward the center of the pizza. If the egg drips off the crust, it's totally fine. You'll just get some crispy bits around the edges.

5. Bake for 25 to 30 minutes or until the crust has started to turn golden and the eggs are your desired doneness; 20 to 25 minutes should get you an over-medium egg.

6. Remove from the oven and let cool for a few minutes on the baking sheet. Garnish with cilantro, cut into slices, and serve. Enjoy!

····· **TIPS** ·····

This recipe uses a decent amount of tomato sauce because I wanted to ensure the eggs didn't fall off the pie. This might be one of those slices that you eat with a fork and knife, and there's no shame in that because it's freaking delicious.

For an extra hit of heat, you can add a little harissa paste to the tomato sauce. It can be hard to find occasionally, so if you can't locate it, you can substitute another chili paste instead.

Keep a watchful eye on those eggs as they cook!

Pear, Prosciutto, & Arugula Pizza

SERVES 4–6 PEOPLE (AND HUNTY, OF COURSE) | PREP TIME: 1 HOUR
TOTAL TIME: 1 HOUR 30 MINUTES

It's giving richhh—you're going to look hot and fancy eating this pie. But also, this pizza is rich in flavor from all the cheese, prosciutto, and walnuts. The bit of sweetness from the figs cuts the fattiness of the cheese, and the arugula adds the perfect bite of freshness. Insert shavings of imaginary truffles and dollops of caviar on top because you're richhh.

1. Preheat the oven to 350°F (180°C).

2. Lightly flour your work surface, and use a rolling pin to roll out the dough to fit the baking sheet you're using. Gently transfer the dough to the baking sheet.

3. Evenly distribute the olive oil and fig jam over the dough, leaving a ½- to 1–inch (1.25–2.5cm) border around the edges. Distribute the garlic, brie, Parmesan, yellow onion, prosciutto, figs, and walnuts in an even layer over the oil and jam.

4. Bake for 25 to 30 minutes or until the crust has started to turn golden.

5. Remove from the oven and let cool for a few minutes on the baking sheet. Top with arugula, drizzle with balsamic glaze, cut into slices and serve. Enjoy!

Sprinkle of all-purpose flour, for dusting

1 pound (450g) Homemade Pizza Dough (see page 210) or store-bought pizza dough

3 tablespoons olive oil

3 tablespoons fig jam (optional)

4–6 garlic cloves, minced

1× 8-ounce (225g) wheel Brie, thinly sliced

½ cup grated Parmesan

1 yellow onion, thinly sliced

3 ounces (85g) prosciutto

5–6 figs, sliced

¼ cup walnuts, halved or roughly chopped

2 cups arugula

Drizzle of balsamic vinegar, for garnish

Special equipment

Rolling pin

> ············ **TIP** ············
>
> I made the fig jam optional because not everyone loves a sweet flavor on pizza. We all know the pineapple-ham controversy!

Sprinkle of all-purpose flour, for dusting

1 pound (450g) Homemade Pizza
Dough (see page 210), store-bought
pizza dough, or lavash

8 ounces (225g) fresh mozzarella, torn
or shredded

1–2 cups rotisserie chicken, cut into
bite-sized pieces or shredded

1 red bell pepper, ribs and seeds
removed and cut into thin slices,
or red chili pepper slices if you like
it spicy

1 red onion, thinly sliced

½ cup shredded carrots

peanuts, roughly chopped, for garnish

Fresh cilantro, roughly chopped,
for garnish

For the sauce

¼–½ cup smooth peanut butter

¼ cup hoisin sauce

2 tablespoons sweet chili sauce

2 tablespoons rice wine vinegar

1 teaspoon ground ginger

1 tablespoon sesame oil

2 tablespoons oyster sauce

2 limes, 1 juiced and 1 cut into wedges,
for garnish

Special equipment

Rolling pin

Thai-Inspired Chicken Pizza

SERVES 4-6 | PREP TIME: 10 MINUTES | TOTAL TIME: 45 MINUTES

This pie is inspired by one of my favorite local pizza places, Rhombus Guys. It's one of the best spots in town to get a decent slice when you've got some cravings after being up to no good for the evening. This recipe can be made using a lavash crust if you like. Lavash is technically a flatbread, but if you are someone who likes a thin, cracker-like crust to your pizza, then you're absolutely going to love lavash. What I love most about it? Besides the crunchy bite, it's a time-saver!

1. Preheat the oven to 350°F (180°C).

2. To make the sauce, in a medium bowl, combine the peanut butter, hoisin sauce, sweet chili sauce, rice wine vinegar, ginger, sesame oil, oyster sauce, and lime juice.

3. If using pizza dough, lightly flour your work surface, and use a rolling pin to roll out the dough to fit the baking sheet you're using. Gently transfer the dough to the baking sheet. (If you're using lavash, place it on the baking sheet.) Evenly spread the sauce over the dough, leaving a ½- to 1-inch (1.25–2.5cm) border around the edges. Distribute the mozzarella, chicken, red pepper, red onion, and carrots evenly over the sauce.

4. Bake for 25 to 30 minutes or until the crust has started to turn golden.

5. Remove from the oven and let cool for a few minutes on the baking sheet. Garnish with peanuts and cilantro, cut into slices, and serve. Enjoy!

Mom's Fruit Pizza

SERVES 8-10 | PREP TIME: 30 MINUTES | TOTAL TIME: 1 HOUR

One of my fondest memories is making fruit pizza with my mom and siblings. When the summer sun is out, I tend to gravitate toward fresh foods and refreshing beverages and desserts. This is a cool dessert, and it's also great alongside the pizzas in this chapter. When I was raising money for bake sales to help my community, this pizza was a big hit. People loved it!

1. Preheat the oven to 350°F (180°C). Line a baking sheet with parchment paper.

2. In a medium bowl, whisk together the butter, brown sugar, granulated sugar, vanilla extract, and almond extract until a sugary paste forms.

3. Add the egg and salt, and whisk well.

4. Add the all-purpose flour, baking powder, and baking soda, and give the dry ingredients a light whisk on top of the wet ingredients before mixing everything together to form a dough.

5. Form the dough into whatever shape you want (I like to make a rainbow), and place it on the prepared baking sheet.

6. Bake for 20 to 25 minutes or until the crust has started to turn golden.

7. Remove from the oven and let cool completely on the pan about 1 hour.

8. Meanwhile, in a small bowl mix together the cream cheese, Greek yogurt, vanilla extract, and confectioners' sugar, if using.

9. When the cookie crust is cool, add the frosting on top, leaving about 1 inch (2.5cm) around the edges of the crust.

10. Using a paper towel, pat dry the blueberries, kiwis, strawberries, pineapple, mandarin oranges, and grapes, and add to the frosting in whatever kind of pattern you'd like—or just slap it all on! Cut into slices, and serve immediately. Enjoy!

For the cookie crust

1 cup unsalted butter, softened

¾ cup lightly packed brown sugar

¼ cup granulated sugar

2 teaspoons vanilla extract

Teeny dash of almond extract (about ¼ teaspoon)

1 large egg

Pinch of salt

1½ cups all-purpose flour

1 teaspoon baking powder

1 teaspoon baking soda

For the toppings

4 ounces (115g) cream cheese (about ½× 8-ounce/225g block)

½ cup Greek yogurt

1 teaspoon vanilla extract

2 tablespoons confectioners' sugar (optional)

1 pint (300g) blueberries or blackberries

2-3 kiwis, thinly sliced

1 pint (475g) strawberries, thinly sliced

½× Fresh Pineapple cut into slices or chunks

1× 15-ounce (425g) can mandarin oranges, drained, or 3 fresh mandarin oranges, peeled and separated into segments

2 ounces (55g) seedless grapes (Red or white (green))

> **TIPS**
>
> Be sure the cut fruit is dry before you place it on the pizza, or the moisture could make the cookie crust soggy.
>
> Try mixing up the fruits you use. Any will work!
>
> Instead of one big fruit pizza, you can make a bunch of little crusts and have the frosting and toppings available for everyone to customize their own pie.
>
> Form the dough to create whatever shape that you want, which can be lots of fun for a theme party. Kids absolutely love it!
>
> This does not have a long fridge life—only one or two days before it gets too soggy—so be sure you eat it relatively quickly!

4

YOU DESERVE A DRINK & A SWEET TREAT

COURAGE

There was a point in my life when I temporarily fell out of love with myself. Sometimes I like to nerd out and pretend as if every day I'm preparing for battle. Forged from the love and courage of the people I care about and who protect me, my armor makes me stronger. It gives me the strength to take on any foe, real or imaginary. I'm proud of my empire and ready to lead onward to victory because love will win. Especially now that I've got so many of you in my corner.

Courage is extremely important, no matter the task. It gives us the strength to try new things, to rise up against things that we find unjust, and to stand out when we are more comfortable blending in. The idea of making a change or taking a risk can be a scary but necessary part of life. How else are you going to follow your dreams?

It takes courage to live the life you want to live. If you feel like you lack courage, I recommend starting with hobbies and things that you really enjoy doing, getting involved in your community, and doing your diligence in society.

It also takes courage to stand up for people. When you see something happening, you should stand up for what you believe in. When you use and apply your skills, you can become your own wizard, conjuring beauty and healing for yourself and for others. Break the curses of your personal oppressors, and live every day genuinely.

Courage also can look like trying new foods, especially if you're a picky eater. It looks different for everyone based on their experiences, and every moment in life adds value to your overall knowledge.

Whatever the day or the future brings, you've got this. You've got that sweet, sweet courage inside, and I believe in you.

HAPPY HOUR

Pear and Basil Mojito

SERVES 4–6 | PREP TIME: 10 MINUTES | TOTAL TIME: 10 MINUTES

Are you one of those people who likes to have three to twelve different beverages in front of you at all times? I know I am. For example, I always have a giant water bottle full of crispy ice water for hydration, a lukewarm coffee with a touch of creamer and cinnamon for focus, a smoothie from breakfast for nourishment, and a Diet Coke for flavor. Sometimes I'll also have an aloe drink because it's interesting, and of course, a cocktail (or mocktail), like this one, to tie off the evening. It soothes me, and I have the most productive days ever!

This cocktail uses canned pears because IDK about you, but whenever I buy a pear in the store, it's always hard and never get soft enough by the time I want to use it. I was also just a weird little kid who liked eating fruit out of a can.

Sugar or salt, for rimming the glasses (optional)

10 fresh basil or mint leaves, or both, plus extra for garnish

¼ cup lime juice, plus extra for rimming the glasses

½ cup lime-flavored rum, or ½ cup lemon-lime soda (for a mocktail)

Juice of 1× 15-ounce (425g) can pears (about 4–6 tablespoons pear juice), fruit reserved for garnish

¼ cup pear-flavored vodka (omit for a mocktail)

Fresh or canned pear slices, for garnish

½ cup cold club soda

Special equipment

Cocktail shaker

Muddler

1. Pour the sugar or salt into a small, shallow dish. Set aside.

2. Add the basil (and/or mint) to a cocktail shaker, and muddle well.

3. Add the lime juice, rum, pear juice, and vodka, and top with ice. Cover the shaker, and shake well.

4. To prep your serving glasses, rub a lemon or pear around each rim and dip into the sugar. Fill the glasses with ice, and strain in the drink.

5. Garnish with fresh basil (and/or mint) and a sliced pear, top with a splash of club soda, and serve. Enjoy—and please drink responsibly!

> ········ **TIPS** ········
>
> You can turn the pear into a fun garnish by cutting out fun shapes with little cookie cutters!
>
> Or precut one slice in the pears so it can hang off your glass or skewers!

1 cup frozen dragon fruit chunks

1 cup fresh mango, roughly chopped, or frozen mango chunks

4 cups cranberry-mango juice

½ cup dragon fruit–flavored rum, lemon-lime soda, or iced green tea

Handful of fresh mint or basil leaves, for garnish

.... **TIP** ....

If you're feeling like going to Margaritaville, add all the fruit and ice to a high-powered blender. Pour in the rum and half of the juice, and blend for 2 minutes. If the blender needs more liquid, add a splash more cranberry-mango juice until you reach your desired texture. Pour into cute glasses, garnish with some mint leaves, and enjoy!

The Dragon Fruit Dehydrator

SERVES 4–6 | PREP TIME: 5 MINUTES | TOTAL TIME: 5 MINUTES

This is inspired by my favorite "not even a coffee" drink (because I barely drink coffee, which shocks so many people!). It's a Starbee's drink, the Dragon Fruit Refresher. I love it so much, but there's never enough juice in the original. For legal and obvious reasons (joking), I've decided to call my version a Dragon Fruit Dehydrator. Please do not drink this on your morning commute.

1. In a pitcher, add the dragon fruit, mango, and 1 cup ice. Add the cranberry-mango juice and rum, and stir.

2. Pour yourself a cute glass, garnish with some fresh mint leaves, and serve. Enjoy—and please drink responsibly!

Pretty in Purple

SERVES 2–4 | PREP TIME: 5 MINUTES | TOTAL TIME:10 MINUTES

"I just want to let them know that they didn't break me" is a line from the film *Pretty in Pink*. I can really appreciate the courage it took for Andie to overcome her struggles when people spoke so poorly of her behind her back. I'm a fan of grabbing a glass of adult candy (alcohol) or a bowl of popcorn, and watching cheesy rom-coms where the main character finds a happy ending with a dreamboat. So this beverage is inspired by one of my favorites, but instead of "Pretty in Pink," I'm calling it "Pretty in Purple." Cheers to everyone else who wears their heart on their sleeves!

1. In a small saucepan over medium-low heat, combine the blueberries, honey, and lemon juice. Cook, stirring, for 8 to 10 minutes. Remove from the heat and set aside to cool completely.

2. In a cocktail shaker, add half of the cooled, strained simple syrup and the pineapple juice. Cover the shaker and mix well.

3. Fill the serving glasses with ice, equally distribute the liquid among the glasses, and add a few chunks of fresh fruit if desired. Pour in some of the tonic water and the Empress 1908 Indigo Gin, and stir for an incredible color combination.

4. Garnish with more fresh berries, and serve. Enjoy—and please drink responsibly!

1 pint (300g) blueberries or blackberries, a small handful reserved for garnish

2 ounces (55) honey

1 ounce (30ml) lemon or lime juice

1 cup pineapple juice or orange juice

1 quart (1 liter) sparkling or tonic water, plus extra to top off the drinks

1½ ounces (45ml) Empress 1908 Indigo Gin (see Tips)

Special equipment

Cocktail shaker

······· **TIP** ·······

Empress 1908 Indigo Gin has a cool effect of changing color when mixed with citrus. When the two liquids combine, the gin changes from a violet to a fuchsia color! To make a nonalcoholic version, brew a cup of butterfly pea flower tea (which is what Empress uses to color its gin), let it cool in the fridge, and then use 1½ ounces (45ml) to make your mocktail.

Aperol Spritz with Olives

SERVES 1 | PREP TIME: 5 MINUTES | TOTAL TIME: 5 MINUTES (OR 45 MINUTES IF YOU'RE FREEZING YOUR ORANGE SLICES)

3 ounces (90ml) sparkling wine
  (I recommend prosecco.)

2 ounces (60ml) Aperol or Liqueur
  de Calamansi

1 ounce (30ml) soda water or club soda

1-2 oranges, thinly sliced

Pitted green olives, for garnish

This was my favorite cocktail before it was cool because you can sip it all day and usually not get too buzzed. Americans (me included) tend to get one thing wrong when it comes to this drink: no olives. Across the ocean, they add olives to the Aperol Spritz, which brings a necessary touch of savoriness. So here's a cheers to my Italian ancestors!

1. In a large wine glass (long or short stem is fine), add the sparkling wine, followed by the Aperol, and then the soda water.

2. Garnish with orange slices (try frozen oranges, see Tip) and green olives, and top with ice. Enjoy—and please drink responsibly!

TIPS

You can freeze the orange slices on a baking sheet so they act as an ice cube in your beverage. Or if they're in season, cut some kumquats in half and freeze them in ice cube trays in place of ice.

Because I know that Aperol sells out often, I wanted to give you more options that I think you will love. If you cannot find Aperol or Calamansi, try St-Germain elderflower liqueur or Luxardo Bitter Bianco.

I wouldn't recommend making this drink in a pitcher in larger amounts because this cocktail is simply better when made fresh. It comes together in a flash so you can make several quickly!

If savory olives aren't your thing, and you like drinks as sweet as you are, try this garnished with a mini scoop of sorbet instead. It's simply delightful!

Hot & Dirty Martini

SERVES 2 (WITH A SHIT TON OF STUFFED OLIVES) | PREP TIME: 10 MINUTES
TOTAL TIME: 10 MINUTES

I like my men like I like my martinis—hot and dirty. I like to believe I'd make a great 1950's-style househusband. That said, I recently saw a list of qualities that were EXPECTED of 1950s housewives. Let's see how well I'd hold up:

1. **Dedicate your day to cleaning the house and taking care of clutter.** *(Yeah, right. I can barely clean the dishes. Plus, I consider myself a bit of a maximalist.)*

2. **Wear a cute outfit.** *(Sure! On special occasions...and if all my sweatpants are dirty).*

3. **Prepare the children.** *(All I can imagine is Kate Hudson's voice in* How to Lose a Guy in 10 Days *saying, "We don't have children!!")*

4. **Be a good listener.** *(I am actually a very good listener, so this one I can manage.)*

5. **Greet your husband with a drink.** *(I can do that, too, and this is the recipe I would make!)*

Let's also remember that women's rights were minimal at this time. I'm definitely not down with that. So here's to change!

1. In a food processor, purée the blue cheese until it's fluffy.

2. Using a small butter knife or an offset spatula, fill the green olives with the fluffy cheese. Set aside.

3. In a cocktail shaker, add 1 cup ice cubes, the vodka, vermouth, and hot sauce, if using. Cover the shaker and mix well.

4. Strain into chilled martini glasses, garnish with some of the olives on a skewer, and serve. Enjoy—and please drink responsibly!

4 ounces (115g) bleu cheese or Boursin

6 ounces (170g) pitted green olives, brine reserved

6-7 ounces (180–208ml) good-quality vodka

2 teaspoons dry vermouth

A couple drops of hot sauce (optional)

Special equipment

Food processor

Cocktail shaker and skewers

Chilled glasses

········· **TIPS** ·········

If you don't love olives, that's totally fine. I got you: you can use pepperoncini or pickled sweet peppers instead. You can even stuff them with the cheese if you want.

Although this recipe makes only two cocktails, it does make a ton of Delishaas stuffed olives that you can serve on a charcuterie board or batter and fry if you're feeling extra!

½ teaspoon celery salt, for rimming the glasses

6 ounces (180ml) vodka of choice

¼ cup pickle brine

1 lemon or lime, half juiced and half cut into wedges, for garnish

3 dashes Worcestershire sauce

½ teaspoon prepared horseradish (optional)

3 dashes hot sauce of choice (or more if you like it extra spicy)

½ teaspoon smoked paprika

½ teaspoon Old Bay Seasoning

1 cup Clamato or tomato soup (I like to use Pacific Foods' Organic Roasted Red Pepper and Tomato Soup)

Rolled prosciutto, pickled Italian vegetables, pitted green olives, pickled sweet peppers, pickled pearl onions, and fresh celery stalks, for garnish (optional)

Special equipment

Cocktail skewers

TIPS

Try this will a fun flavored vodka, like pickle-infused, garlic-infused, or bacon-infused!

Pair with a light beer chaser and some Dive Bar Buffalo Wings (see page 61).

Loaded Bloody Mary

SERVES 2-4 | PREP TIME: 5 MINUTES | TOTAL TIME: 5 MINUTES

When I was in college working three jobs to pay off my tuition tab for the semester, along with my rent, one of my jobs was as a server at a trendy chain restaurant known for their Texas-sized combos, ice-cold beers, margs, and warm buns served with honey cinnamon butter. You could catch me violently hungover every Sunday morning after drinking box wine and watching scary movies the night before with my best friend and at-the-time roommate, Jessica. Such Sundays were also known as "Bloody Sundays." On those Bloody Sundays I had to work, I would line dance and shout birthday wishes to little kids, and to the whole restaurant. This is ode to when I mastered making bloody Mary's...and line dancing!

1. Pour the celery salt into a small, shallow dish. Set aside.

2. Fill a large pitcher with at least 2½ cups ice cubes, add the vodka, pickle brine, juice if ½ lemon, Worcestershire sauce, horseradish, hot sauce, smoked paprika, Old Bay Seasoning, and Clamato, and mix well.

3. To prep your serving glasses, rub a wedge of lemon around each rim and dip into the celery salt. Fill the glasses with fresh ice, and pour in the drink.

4. Garnish with skewers of rolled prosciutto, pickled Italian vegetables, pitted green olives, pickled sweet peppers, or pickled pearl onions, if using. Finish with a lime wedge and a fresh celery stalk, and serve. Enjoy—and please drink responsibly!

Strip & Go Naked

SERVES 10-12 | PREP TIME: 5 MINUTES | TOTAL TIME: 5 MINUTES

This is a drink for floating down the river. If you've never gone on a float before, it is a magical summer tradition where you float in an inner tube down the largest body of water you can find. There's usually a car with a designated driver at the end who drives you back to the start to float down again. You drink cocktails as you float along, and because you've been sitting for so long, you don't know how drunk you are. So please, drink responsibly! And drink some water!

This is going to sound a little trashy, but when you're on the river, you're not allowed to bring glass bottles, for obvious reasons, so you'll need a big, VERY FRESHLY CLEANED cooler in which to serve this elevated beverage. Even better if it has a spout dispenser. And don't forget that the beverage cooler gets its own inner tube—and that you have to tie it down realllllll good like.

1. Pour the beer, peach concentrate, and vodka into a clean cooler, and mix well.

2. Stir in the frozen peach slices along with some ice.

3. Pour a glass over ice, garnish with a gummy peach ring for a little bit of sour, and serve. Enjoy—and please drink responsibly!

6 pack of light beer

1× 12-ounce can orange juice or lemonade concentrate

6-12 ounces (180-355ml) peach-flavored vodka

1 pound (450g) frozen peach slices

Sweet-and-sour gummy peach rings, for garnish (optional)

Special equipment:

Cooler

········· **TIPS** ·········

To make this a mocktail, substitute non alcoholic ginger beer (or your choice nonalcoholic beer) or sparkling water for the alcoholic beer and peach iced tea for the vodka.

This drink is very interchangeable, and you can swap out the concentrate and frozen fruit with whatever flavors you're craving. Sometimes I make it with lemonade concentrate. But I highly recommend trying the original first!

1 cup pineapple juice, divided

2 cups orange juice, divided

4 cups cranberry juice or grape juice, divided

8 ounces (238ml) fruit-flavored vodka ((prefer raspberry for this)

1 quart (1 liter) ginger ale or lemon-lime soda, use the remaining to top off the beverage

A couple scoops of sherbet and a variety of mixed fruit or fresh herbs, for garnish (I used cranberry, mixed berries, and rosemary)

Special equipment

Punch bowl and ladle

Ice mold (or Bundt pan)

········ **TIPS** ·········

You can use leftover fruit from one of the other recipes in this book as a garnish, or buy a bag of frozen mixed berries.

The fruit dip recipe (see page 35) and Mom's Fruit Pizza (see page 228) go very well alongside this punch.

Graduation Punch

SERVES 8-10 | PREP TIME: 5 MINUTES | TOTAL TIME: 5 HOURS

I'm not entirely sure if this recipe exists outside my family, but at just about every graduation party, we serve this punch. The hallmark of the beverage was originally a combination of Hawaiian Punch and Sprite that would be frozen in a Bundt pan to create a giant ice ring. I made this spiked version so no one had to "accidentally" spike it, so cheers to you on graduating!

1. In a punch bowl or pitcher, combine the pineapple juice, orange juice, and cranberry juice. Top it off with ginger ale. Pop it in the fridge so it's cold when you're ready to serve.

2. Fill the ice mold with a handful of fruit, followed by ¼ cup of the drink mixture, then half of the remaining fruit of choice and herbs. Fill the rest with water, leaving about 1 inch from the top, so that there's room for it to freeze and expand.

3. Place the ice mold in the freezer for at least 1-2 hours or until partially frozen, Remove from the freezer. Add the remaining fruit garnish to the top, then pop it back in the freezer for 3-4 hours or until frozen solid.

4. Pop the ice out of the mold, into your serving bowl followed by the beverage, which will make it float. Add the sherbet and any remaining fruit and serve. Enjoy—and please drink responsibly!

Sangria Spritzer

SERVES 4–6 | PREP TIME: 10 MINUTES | TOTAL TIME: 20 MINUTES

Sangria is truly one of my favorite summer beverages. It makes me think of "Honey, I'm Home" by Shania Twain. The vibe is I just got home, give the dog a bone, I gotta get off my feet, give me something to eat, pour me a cold one. Hard day of work or not, give me a sangria.

I think you'll agree this is the fruit punch of wines. It's like a whole fruit salad in a bottle and then you add even more fruit that you can snack on while you sip with the ghouls on your patio while we spill the tea and work on tanning our legs pretending were on an island in the sun. Then you literally look like the Martha Stewart of your friend group because you effortlessly threw together this cocktail (or mocktail). Look at you. The hostess with the mostess!

1. In a large pitcher, combine the grapefruit, orange, lemon, lime, and sugar and let them macerate (draw out the liquid from the citrus) for about 5 to 10 minutes.

2. Add the raspberries, strawberries, cherries, and blackberries, and top with the sangria and sparkling wine.

3. Pop into the refrigerator to chill for 10 minutes, and serve. Enjoy—and please drink responsibly! (And snack on the fruit while you drink!)

1 grapefruit, thinly sliced

1 navel orange, thinly sliced

1 lemon, thinly sliced

1 lime, thinly sliced

1 tablespoon turbinado sugar

½ cup raspberries

½ cup strawberries, thinly sliced

½ cup fresh cherries, pitted (maraschino cherries also work)

½ cup blackberries

1× 25-ounce (750ml) bottle sangria or low-sugar fruit punch, chilled

½× 25-ounce (750ml) bottle sparkling wine or nonalcoholic sparkling grape juice (white or red)

TIP

You can make your sangria quicker if you start with chilled fruits and liquids. I would still recommend that you let everything macerate in step 1, but you can skip the chilling in step 3 if everything is cold before you begin. Or try using some frozen fruits!

2 cups sugar

7½ cups water, divided

1 cup pomegranate juice

2-3 ripe star fruits

3 lemons or limes, 2 juiced and 1 sliced into rounds

1 pomegranate, arils removed

Special equipment

Punch bowl

Star Fruit & Pomegranate Lemonade

SERVES 6-8 | PREP TIME: 10 MINUTES | TOTAL TIME: 10 MINUTES

When I talk about how much I love star fruit, I feel like I have my own TV show and I'm explaining the shape, flavor, and uniqueness of this exotic fruit and how happy I am to have found it in the frozen tundra I inhabit. I remember the first time I saw a starfruit; I was so impressed by not only the flavor but also the shape. When developing this cocktail, I thought star fruit slices would look stunning lining a giant pitcher full of a refreshing beverage.

I have a full bowl of lemons in my apartment at all times (not like the fake ones you might have seen in *Architectural Digest* ...), and they are by far one of the most used ingredients in my kitchen. If I were to open a lemonade stand, this is what I would serve and we would only play Beyoncé's *Lemonade* album. So okay ladies, now let's get in formation...

1. In a medium pan over medium heat, combine the sugar with 1½ cups water and the pomegranate juice. Bring to a light simmer, and stir until the sugar is dissolved. Remove from the heat and set aside to cool.

2. Cut off the tops and the bottoms of the star fruits, and slice into star-shaped rounds. Set aside.

3. In a punch bowl or pitcher, add the remaining 6 cups of water and then stir in the lemon juice. Add the cooled pomegranate simple syrup to your desired sweetness level, and mix again.

4. Stir in the star fruit and pomegranate arils along with the pomegranate juice.

5. Pop into the refrigerator to cool until ready to serve. Add some ice and serve. Enjoy—and please drink responsibly!

LET THEM EAT CAKE & COOKIES... & ICE CREAM, TOO!

Cherry Surprise

SERVES 6-8 | PREP TIME: 10 MINUTES | TOTAL TIME:1 HOUR (UP TO OVERNIGHT)

This recipe used to be based on an old Betty Crocker dump cake recipe—that name sounds unappealing, but I assure you, it's delicious.

I am still under the impression that my mom invented dump cake. She didn't, but I like to pretend she did. As a kid, describing my favorite dessert to other kids, I didn't quite know how to explain this dessert other than being like cherry pie, but better! This version is more of an elevated dump cake! If you want to make it the traditional way, see the Tips.

1. In a large saucepan over medium-low heat, combine the cherries, lemon juice, granulated sugar, almond flour, almond extract, vanilla extract, and butter. Bring to a light simmer or boil for about 6 to 8 minutes or until thick. Remove from the heat, and set aside to cool.

2. In the bowl of a stand mixer fitted with the paddle attachment, add the cream cheese and confectioners' sugar, and mix on low to medium for about 5 minutes. Remove the bowl from the mixer and fold in the whipped topping and the angel food cake using a spatula.

3. In a trifle dish, or the serving dish of your choice, assemble the dessert, starting with a layer of the cherry filling on the bottom, followed by a couple scoops of the creamy cake mix. Repeat the layers until you're out of both. Pop this into the refrigerator for at least an hour to set up until ready to serve. For the best results, store the dessert in an air-tight container in the fridge. It will stay fresh for 5 to 6 days.

For the filling

4 cups cherries, pitted, or 3× 21-ounce (600g) cans cherry pie filling

Juice of ½ lemon

½ cup granulated sugar

2 tablespoons almond flour or cornstarch

¼ teaspoon almond extract

1 teaspoon vanilla extract

2 tablespoons unsalted butter

For the topping

2× 8-ounce (225g) blocks cream cheese

¼ cup confectioners' sugar

1× 8-ounce (225g) container frozen whipped topping, thawed

1 store-bought angel food cake, cut into bite-sized pieces

Special equipment

Stand mixer with a paddle attachment

Trifle dish

········· **TIPS** ··········

If you want to make this the way I did when I was a kid, you can use two cans of cherry pie filling (instead of making your own cherry filling mixture) with a yellow cake mix topped with 8 tablespoons of unsalted butter and bake at 350°F (180°C) for 35 to 40 minutes or until browned on top. This also saves you a TON of time.

You can make your own whipped cream by adding 2 cups of heavy cream and ¼ cup of confectioners' sugar to a stand mixer fitted with the whisk attachment. Whip on medium until soft peaks form.

1× 14-ounce (400g) can sweetened
   condensed milk

½ tablespoon vanilla extract or vanilla
   bean paste

2 cups heavy whipping cream

1× 8-ounce (225g) container frozen
   whipped topping,. thawed

Optional mix-ins

1-2 cups roughly chopped cookies
   (about 8-10 cookies)

Brownie or blondie chunks

Leftover cheesecake bites

Berries

Chocolate and/or candy bar chunks

Sprinkles (As many as you feel
   are necessary)

Special equipment

Stand mixer with a whisk attachment
   or an electric hand mixer

9×5-inch (23×12.5cm) loaf pan or
   freezer-safe container, cold

········· **TIPS** ·········

Be sure your mixer and
the bowl you are going
to put the ice cream in
are cold. I'M SERIOUS.
Put those bowls in the
fridge or freezer. It will
make a difference!

Lately I've been adding
crumbled sugar cones,
honey, or culinary dried
lavender to my ice
cream. Don't be afraid
to lean into some floral
flavors.

You can dress this
recipe up by drizzling in
some of your favorite
chocolate or caramel
sauce halfway through
freezing. Add a design
by running a skewer
through the sauce, or
layering it throughout.

No-Churn Ice Cream

SERVES 8–10 | PREP TIME: 10 MINUTES | TOTAL TIME: 6 HOURS (UP TO OVERNIGHT)

No, I unfortunately am not the heir to Häagen-Dazs, but sometimes when I'm in a self-deprecating mood, I have been known to call myself "Hoggin' Haas." If it were up to me, I would eat ice cream for every meal of the day—and I do, sometimes. At other times, I'll sneak into the freezer for a spoonful of something sweet late at night while I dance in the refrigerator light.

You're welcome to make fun of me for loving vanilla ice cream over most other flavors, but I like to use it as a base for mixing in any leftover baked goods I have. Once you've become a master of the original recipe, you can innovate from there. Make a Neapolitan batch! Make a chocolate lover's batch! Just like you and everything you do in life, the options are limitless!

1. Place the 9×5-inch (23×12.5cm) loaf pan or freezer-safe container you want to put your finished ice cream in in the freezer to chill while you make the ice cream. If using a metal pan, line it with parchment paper.

2. In a large metal bowl, add the condensed milk and the vanilla extract. Using a hand mixer with the whisk attachment, whip the mixture for a minute or so.

3. To the bowl of a stand mixer, add the heavy whipping cream. Whip on medium-high for about 5 to 7 minutes or until you get about stiff peaks.

4. Using a rubber spatula, fold in half of the sweetened condensed milk mixture and half of the whipped topping. When that's combined, add in whatever mix-ins you'd like.

5. Fold in the remaining sweetened milk and whipped topping. The mixture will have a super light and fluffy feeling.

6. Remove the container from the freezer and load it up with the ice cream mix.

7. Pop the dish back into the freezer, and freeze overnight, or for 6 to 12 hours for best results. Store the ice cream in a covered container in the freezer for up to one month.

S'mores Chocolate Chip Cookies

SERVES 12–15 MEDIUM-SIZED COOKIES | PREP TIME: 5 MINUTES | TOTAL TIME: 25 MINUTES

I love living in an apartment building for a couple reasons: I do not have to shovel my own sidewalk, and I don't have to worry about too much food waste because all my neighbors will take my creations off my hands. Every time someone new moves into the building, I usually welcome them with a plate of cookies. These are like s'mores cookies. They remind me so much of Wisconsin, so it's always nice to share a little piece of home with a new friend! This is my Mr. Rogers friendly reminder, to say, "Howdy neighbor," and leave a cute note. A great and easy way to share some cookies and make a friend!

1. Preheat the oven to 375°F (190°C). Line a baking sheet with parchment paper.

2. In a medium bowl, whisk together the butter, brown sugar, granulated sugar, vanilla extract, and almond extract for about 4 minutes or until it becomes a sugary paste.

3. Add the egg and salt, and whisk to combine.

4. Add the all-purpose flour, baking powder, and baking soda on top of the wet ingredients, and give them a light mix to be sure the baking soda and powder are evenly distributed before incorporating.

5. When the dough has come together, add all the mix-ins, and stir to distribute.

6. Scoop out the cookies onto the prepared baking sheet about 1 or 2 inches (2.5–5cm) apart. (They will spread!)

7. Bake for 12 minutes, my lucky number. If your oven cooks unevenly like mine, rotate the baking sheet halfway through the cook time. Check for doneness—they should look a little golden and not too wet. Remove from the oven and sprinkle each cookie with a teeny pinch of flaky salt.

8. Let the cookies cool completely on the baking sheet before serving. Store the cookies in an air-tight container for up to one week.

1 cup unsalted butter, softened

¾ cup lightly packed brown sugar

¼ cup granulated sugar

2 teaspoons vanilla extract

Teeny dash of almond extract (about ¼ teaspoon)

1 large egg

Pinch of salt

1½ cups all-purpose flour

1 teaspoon baking powder

1 teaspoon baking soda

Flaky salt, for garnish

Mix-ins

½ cup mini marshmallows or marshmallow fluff

½ cup chocolate chips

6 sugar cones (the waffle kind), crushed (optional)

TIPS

For even chocolatier cookies, add ½ cup unsweetened cocoa powder to the dry ingredients in step 4.

Use an ice cream scoop to measure your dough and plop it onto the baking sheet. You'll be pleased that the cookies turn out to be evenly sized.

A lot of people need to chill their dough. I specifically tested this recipe a million times to avoid that requirement. However, if you live or work in a hot kitchen or even a hot place on this floating planet, it's probably going to work better for you if you chill the dough for at least an hour. So if you need to make these in batches, refrigerate the dough when you're not using it.

You can use marshmallows in the batter or arrange them on top. The marshmallow gets like little crunchy pockets within the cookie when it cools—arguably some of the best parts of the cookie. But you can arrange them on top; these cookies spread very easily because of the butter and sugar content.

Hazelnut & Cookie Butter Milkshakes

SERVES 2 | PREP TIME: 5 MINUTES | TOTAL TIME:10 MINUTES

1 pint (16 ounces/475ml) No-Churn Ice Cream (see page 26) or store-bought ice cream, any flavor

¼ cup cookie butter

¼ cup hazelnut butter or spread

2 tablespoons malted milk powder (optional)

½ cup milk of choice

Handful crumbled Biscoff cookies (optional)

Whipped cream, maraschino cherries (with the stem), sprinkles, extra crumbled Biscoff cookies, or Fruity Pebbles for cereal flavor, for garnish (optional)

Special equipment

High-powered blender

My milkshake brings all the men to the yard, and they're like, it's better than yours. I can teach you, but I have to charge. (But you already paid because you're reading this.) With the combination of cookie butter and quite literally anything else, I would also dance seductively and attract the attention of male suitors to the yard. You'll understand when you suck it down. And can you tie a cherry stem with your tongue? I can.

1. In a high-powered blender, add the No-Churn Ice Cream first, followed by the cookie butter, hazelnut butter, malted milk powder, and a splash of milk. Blend. If it's not coming together nicely, slowly add a little more milk until it's your desired texture. This should only take 1 or 2 minutes.

2. If you want, you can add a handful of some crumbled Biscoff cookies to the mix at this point for some more lumps and chewable bites. Blend the mixture again to distribute the cookies.

3. Pour the milkshake into one or two serving glasses. Garnish with whipped cream, maraschino cherries, sprinkles, and cookies or cereal, if you like. Add a straw (or two if you feel like sharing), and serve. Enjoy immediately.

> **TIPS**
>
> Serve with some french fries for dipping, and pretend you're on a diner date.
>
> Alexa, play "Milkshake" by Kelis. La la la la and warm it up. La la la la laa. Soften the ice cream on the counter for a few minutes before you attempt to scoop it out.
>
> You can use whatever type of ice cream you like for this, but keep in mind that the better the quality of the ice cream, the better the quality of the milkshake.

Bella's No-Bake Cheesecake

SERVES 6-8 | PREP TIME: 30 MINUTES | TOTAL TIME: 1 HOUR 5 MINUTES
(PLUS 5 HOURS TO OVERNIGHT FOR CHILLING)

Everyone should know how to make a no-bake cheesecake. And no, we don't need to bring up the fact that my family is from Wisconsin and loves cheese again. No matter where you're from, sometimes you just need a good slice of cheesecake. More importantly, my little sister's favorite treat is cheesecake. I believe it was originally a Greek dessert that made its way to NYC and then earned its "New York–style cheesecake" moniker. This version isn't quite like that because were not baking it. Technically, you could even make this in a dorm room if you have a big enough fridge!

1. Line a springform pan with parchment paper.

2. In a medium bowl, whisk together the crumbled graham crackers, nutmeg, cinnamon, and granulated sugar. Add the melted butter, and use a rubber spatula to combine. Add the crust mixture to the prepared springform pan, distribute and press the crust evenly along the bottom. Set in the refrigerator to chill for 20 minutes while you make the filling.

3. In a large bowl, and using a mixer on low, beat together the cream cheese, whipped topping, vanilla extract, confectioners' sugar, salt, and half of the sweetened condensed milk for 6 minutes or until halfway combined. Add the remaining condensed milk, and whip for 6 minutes more or until smooth and no lumps remain.

4. In a small pot over medium heat, add the blackberries, lemon juice, and granulated sugar. Cook for about 10 minutes or until you hear the berries start to simmer. You want them only halfway broken down, not turned into a jelly! Let cool for 3 minutes.

5. Add the cream cheese mixture to the crust, then gently pour the berry mixture directly on top of the cheesecake filling, and use a skewer to swirl or mix into your desired pattern.

6. Chill for at least 3 hours and preferably 4 or 5 (or even overnight) before serving. Store the cheesecake in an air-tight container in the fridge for up to one week.

For the crust

2 sleeves of graham crackers, crushed

A heavy pinch of nutmeg

1 teaspoon ground cinnamon

3 tablespoons granulated sugar

8 tablespoons unsalted butter, melted

For the filling

4× 8-ounce (225g) blocks cream cheese

1× 8-ounce (225g) container frozen whipped topping, thawed

½ tablespoon vanilla extract

¼ cup confectioners' sugar

Pinch of salt

½× 14-ounce (400g) can sweetened condensed milk, or 1 cup sour cream

2 pints (510g) blackberries or berry of choice

Juice of 1 lemon

3 tablespoons granulated sugar

Special equipment

9-inch (24cm) springform pan

Electric hand mixer

> ·········· **TIP** ··········
>
> Be sure your filling ingredients are cold before mixing. Think about the cheesecake filling as almost a really, really thick frosting.

Rhubarb Crisp

MAKES 6–12 BARS | PREP TIME: 25 MINUTES | TOTAL TIME: 1 HOUR (PLUS 2–3 HOURS COOLING TIME)

3 cups fresh rhubarb (about 1 pound/450g), cut into 1–2-inch (2½–5cm) pieces

1¼ cups sugar

Zest from ½ lemon (save the juice for the syrup)

½ teaspoon rose water (optional)

1 pound (450g) store-bought phyllo dough, thawed

1 cup unsalted butter, melted

Crushed pistachios and dried rose petals, for garnish

For the syrup

1 cup water

1 cup sugar

½ cup honey

Juice of 1 lemon

Serve with

1 scoop really good vanilla ice cream

Special equipment

Pastry brush

Food processor with the blade attachment

We have some of the most beautiful summers in the upper Midwest. I LOVE it when the plants are in full bloom. When I was a kid, I would scamper around outside in my mom's garden and occasionally sneak a stick of rhubarb or honeysuckle to snack on. But be sure never to eat the leaf from the rhubarb plant because it's not edible! During rhubarb season, there is an abundance of rhubarb, and we are always trying to find new ways to enjoy it. That's how I developed this recipe, which is a twist on a traditional crisp. This is what would happen if baklava came to visit the Midwest!

1. Preheat the oven to 350°F (180°C). Coat a 9×13-inch (23×33cm) baking dish with butter.

2. In a food processor, blend the rhubarb, sugar, lemon zest, and rose water, if using, for 3 to 4 minutes or until finely chopped. Set aside.

3. Line the bottom of the prepared baking dish with one layer of phyllo dough. Butter the phyllo dough using a pastry brush and then add another layer of dough. Repeat this process until you have 8 to 10 layers of phyllo, buttering between each layer, down before adding the filling. This is the bottom layer of crust.

4. Spread a few spoonfuls of the filling in a thin layer over the phyllo. Add two or three sheets of phyllo, brushing on butter between each layer, and then another thin layer of filling. Repeat this until all the filling is gone. For the top layer of the baklava, add the remaining sheet.

5. Cut the baklava into 12–24 little squares (whatever shape pattern you would like to serve), cutting about 75 percent of the way down through the dessert to the bottom of the pan.

6. Bake for 30 to 5 minutes or until golden brown and crispy looking. Remove from the oven to cool.

7. Meanwhile, in a medium saucepan over medium-high heat, bring 1 cup water, the sugar, honey, and lemon juice to a boil. Reduce the heat to low and simmer for 6 to 8 minutes. Remove from the heat, and let the syrup cool.

8. While the baklava is still warm, gently pour the syrup over the top. Let the baklava cool completely before serving. This could take 2 or 3 hours (you can eat it warm but the flavors settles when it cools.)

9. Garnish with some crushed pistachios, rose petals, and ice cream, and serve. Store the crisp in an air-tight container for up to one week.

My BFF's Raspberry Lemon Bars

SERVES 8-12 | PREP TIME: 15 MINUTES | TOTAL TIME: 55 MINUTES (PLUS 20 MINUTES TO COOL)

Ring the church bell because this is another recipe I religiously make for my friends. This is Mary Fontes' recipe (my friend Jessica's mom, my second mother, whom I call "Mama Fontes"). I'll be honest, lemon bars aren't normally my favorite, but I love making these for Jessica because they are her favorite. When Jess and I were roommates for a couple years in college, her mom would drop these lemon bars off as "brain food" for studying. She has always taken the best care of both of us. I know you'll enjoy them, too!

For the crust

1 cup unsalted butter

2 cups all-purpose flour

½ cup confectioners' sugar, plus extra for garnish

For the filling

1 cup granulated sugar

1 cup confectioners' sugar

1 teaspoon baking powder

5-6 tablespoons all-purpose flour

Pinch of salt

Zest and juice of 2 large lemons

4 large eggs

1 × 6-ounce (170g) package fresh raspberries

Crushed freeze-dried raspberries, for garnish

Special equipment

9-inch (24cm) tart pan (optional)

1. Preheat the oven to 350°F (180°C). Lightly coat a 9-inch (24cm) tart pan or 9x13-inch (24×33cm) baking dish with cooking spray.

2. In a small pan over low to medium heat, add the butter and brown for about 5 to 8 minutes. Remove from the heat, and cool for 3 or 4 minutes.

3. In a medium bowl, add the browned butter, all-purpose flour, and confectioners' sugar, and mix until a soft dough comes together. Press the crust mixture into the bottom of the prepared tart pan or baking dish. Bake for 10 to 15 minutes, and set aside to cool.

4. Meanwhile, in a large bowl, add the granulated sugar, confectioners' sugar, baking powder, all-purpose flour, and salt.

5. In a medium bowl, whisk together the lemon zest, lemon juice, and eggs. Add to the dry ingredients, and mix until it feels like a thick soup.

6. Fold in the raspberries, and pour over the baked crust.

7. Bake for 25 to 30 minutes or until the top has a golden crust. Remove from the oven and let cool for 20 minutes.

8. Remove from the tart pan, if using; garnish the lemon bars with the dried raspberries and confectioners' sugar, and serve. Store the bars in an air-tight container for up to one week.

> ·········· **TIP** ··········
>
> If using a tart dish, be sure the pan is greased well so the lemon bars come out easily!

My Best Friends' Wedding Cake

SERVES 6-8 AS A LAYER CAKE OR 24 CUPCAKES | PREP TIME: 20 MINUTES | TOTAL TIME: 1 HOUR 30 MINUTES

I was asked by some of my very best friends, Mary and Adam, to have the honor of baking their wedding day desserts, and of course I said yes! They wanted to do kind of a rustic concept with their cakes, which was totally doable for me. The biggest challenge was going to be the number of cupcakes (they needed more than 600!). But as Lady Gaga once said in a motivational speech, "People can do hard things, and I encourage you to be kind." I was determined to do just that.

With the help of my little sister, I decorated three wedding cakes, 300 regular-sized cupcakes, and 300 mini cupcakes. They were a massive hit, with not a crumb left. This cake in particular was a big, big hit—I am not joking when I tell you that 30 people asked me for this recipe that night. And now I have the pleasure of sharing it with you!

For the cake

Cooking spray or unsalted butter, for greasing

3 cups cake flour

½ teaspoon ground cardamom

Heavy pinch of nutmeg

2 teaspoons pumpkin pie spice

¼ teaspoon ground ginger

¼ teaspoon ground cloves

1½ teaspoons baking soda

1½ teaspoons baking powder

8 tablespoons unsalted butter

1 cup lightly packed dark brown sugar

½ cup granulated sugar

1 cup sour cream

1 tablespoon vanilla extract

2 eggs

½ cup milk of choice

For the frosting

1 cup unsalted butter

1× 8-ounce (225g) block cream cheese

1 teaspoon vanilla extract

Dash of ground cinnamon (optional)

1 cup confectioners' sugar

Drizzle of caramel and toasted coconut, for garnish (optional)

Special equipment

Stand mixer with the paddle attachment

3× 8- or 9-inch (20 or 23cm) cake pans

1. Preheat the oven to 350°F (180°C). Prepare some cut parchment and lightly spray the pan with cooking oil or lightly grease with butter.

2. In a large bowl, combine the cake flour, cardamom, nutmeg, pumpkin pie spice, ginger, cloves, baking soda, and baking powder.

3. In the bowl of a stand mixer with the paddle attachment, cream together the butter, brown sugar, granulated sugar, and sour cream. Add the vanilla extract, eggs, and milk in two or three parts while continuing to mix.

4. Slowly incorporate the dry ingredients into the wet mixture, and continue to mix.

5. Evenly distribute the batter among the prepared cake pans, and bake for up to 40 to 45 minutes or until golden brown but also spongy-looking. Insert a toothpick into the center of each cake; if it comes out clean, the cake is done.

6. Remove from the oven and let the cakes rest in the pans for about 10 minutes before removing them to a wire rack to cool completely. You want fully cooled cakes (you can pop them in the freezer if needed!) because you're doing a cream cheese frosting, and the layers will slide clean off the base faster than a kid on a Slip 'N Slide if your cakes are still warm.

7. Wash the stand mixer bowl and the paddle attachment before making the frosting. To the bowl, add the butter, cream cheese, vanilla extract, cinnamon, and confectioners' sugar. Whip on medium for about 10 to 15 minutes or until creamy.

8. When the cakes have completely cooled, even out your cakes, trim any bumps on top, and eat those (THEY ARE THE BEST PART) so they are flat on top and can stack uniformly. Using a knife or offset spatula, frost the cakes, evenly distributing the frosting among the layers with a light coat on the outside.

9. Garnish with a drizzle of caramel and sprinkle with coconut, if using, and serve. Store the cake in an air-tight container in the fridge for up to one week.

> ·············· **TIPS** ··············
>
> To evenly distribute the batter among the cake pans so your cakes end up all the same size, I recommend using a ladle. It's so easy to keep track of how much batter is being added to each pan. Two or three ladles per pan is about the perfect amount .
>
> I love to bake my cakes and then, when they've cooled, wrap them in plastic wrap and pop them in the freezer until I'm ready to frost them. This way, the crumb coat (the first layer) sticks so much better to the cake without pulling off many crumbs!
>
> For a delicious pumpkin-flavored cake, replace the sour cream with 1 cup pumpkin purée!
>
> Frost a light coat (a crumb coat), after you've frozen the cake, the frosting will stick better! So do a light layer on everything to hold it all together then chill the cake again, then come in for real frosting, it doesn't have to be perfect.
>
> This cake is very moist, so if you don't want to frost it completely it looks great naked! I love to load the frosting into a piping bag along with your piping tip of choice, and pipe the frosting in between the layers.

Brookie Bars

SERVES 12-16 BROWNIES (DEPENDS ON HOW BIG YOU LIKE YOUR BROWNIES)
PREP TIME: 10 MINUTES | TOTAL TIME: 1 HOUR

Apologies if you've heard me say this before, but although I don't like cake all that much, I LOVE brownies. I love brownies so much, in fact, that I purposely never make them because I know we (the brownies and I) would end up like *Titanic*—in a passionate love affair that would lead to me drowning (and I'm too afraid of confrontation so I most likely would offer the door to someone else to float on). All I'm saying is that I would happily paint these brownies like a nude French woman, dripping with chocolate in a saucy portrait to be lost to the depths of the Atlantic Ocean forever.

If you've tried my Hazelnut Cookie Butter Milkshakes (see page 265), you're going to recognize these flavors immediately!

1. Preheat the oven to 350°F (180°C). Lightly coat a 9×13-inch (23×33cm) baking dish with cooking spray, and line it with greased parchment paper.

2. Begin by making the cookie batter. In the bowl of a stand mixer fitted with the paddle attachment, beat the butter, brown sugar, granulated sugar, vanilla extract, and almond extract until no lumps remain. Add the egg, salt, all-purpose flour, baking powder, and baking soda, and mix for 3 or 4 minutes. Stir in the chocolate chips using a rubber spatula.

3. Press the mixture into the bottom of the prepared baking dish and set aside.

4. Wash the stand mixer bowl, and make the brownie batter. Add the hazelnut butter, peanut butter, vanilla extract, eggs, and butter to the bowl of the stand mixer fitted with the whisk attachment, and whisk for 3 to 4 minutes until smooth.

5. Pour in the all-purpose flour, baking powder, and salt, and whisk for about 2 more minutes or until no flour shows. Stir in half of the M&M's, and pour the batter into the prepared baking dish on top of the cookie batter.

6. Cover with foil and bake for 30 minutes.

7. Remove the brookies from the oven. Remove the foil, quickly add the remaining M&M's over the top, and return to the oven. Bake, uncovered, for 15 to 20 more minutes.

8. Remove from the oven, and let cool completely for best results. When it's cool, the brookie should lift right out of the pan. Cut into whatever size feels appropriate to you, and serve. Store the brownies in an air-tight container for up to one week.

For the cookie layer

Cooking spray, for greasing

¾ cup unsalted butter, plus extra for greasing, softened

¼ cup lightly packed brown sugar

¼ cup granulated sugar

2 teaspoons vanilla extract

Teeny dash of almond extract (about ¼ teaspoon)

1 large egg

Pinch of salt

1¼ cups all-purpose flour

1 teaspoon baking powder

1 teaspoon baking soda

½ cup milk chocolate chips

For the brownie layer

1¼ cups hazelnut butter

⅓ cup creamy peanut butter (NOT NATURAL)

2 teaspoons vanilla extract

2 eggs

4 tablespoons unsalted butter, at room temperature or melted

1 cup all-purpose flour, sifted

1 teaspoon baking powder

Pinch of salt

1 cup M&M's, or 1 chocolate bar of your choice, cut into pieces (optional)

Special equipment

Stand mixer with paddle and whisk attachments

9×13-inch (23×33cm) baking dish

> ·················· **TIPS** ··················
>
> If you aren't a peanut butter fan, you can replace it with more hazelnut butter or cookie butter. However, if you are using peanut butter, be sure it's not a natural kind with oil. I've made this mistake because that's what I normally have in my pantry, but it will add too much oil to the brownie mixture.
>
> The brookies are probably best when they're cool. That way the chocolate has gotten to know itself. But you could totally eat them warm if you dare!

.... TIPS ....

When sprayed on baking pans, cooking spray can brown the outsides of light-colored cakes. We're making chocolate, so we don't have to worry about that. But just FYI.

When I was testing this cake, I accidentally ran out of cream as I was making my frosting. If you find yourself in that situation, add about ½ cup of your favorite ice cream to the mix, and you've got an ice cream buttercream frosting!

Birthday Cake Remix

SERVES 6–12 SLICES (DEPENDING ON HOW YOU SLICE THE CAKE)
PREP TIME: 10 MINUTES | TOTAL TIME: 1 HOUR

My little brother, Xavier, is actually quite the little cheffy chef himself, and he helps me come up with lots of my ideas. He doesn't care much for baking, so he challenged me to make his favorite cake, which just so happens to be a BTSC (better than s*x cake). Very interesting name, I know.

This was a fun challenge for me to figure out how to get everything to work correctly. I love this cake because it's soft and moist and doesn't have any bullshit grocery store frosting that dyes your mouth an unnatural color. I think you're going to love this cake in part for how oh so soft and pillowy it melts in your mouth.

For the cake

Cooking spray, for greasing

¾ cup unsalted butter, plus extra for greasing, softened

2 cups granulated sugar

½ cup vegetable oil

3 large eggs, at room temperature

2½ cups all-purpose flour or cake flour

2½ teaspoons baking powder

2½ teaspoons baking soda

1 cup unsweetened cocoa powder

Pinch of salt

1¾ cups buttermilk

2 teaspoons vanilla extract

For the frosting

1× 8-ounce (225g) block cream cheese, softened (optional)

1 cup unsalted butter

½ cup homemade or store-bought caramel sauce (optional) reserve the rest for decorating

2 teaspoons vanilla extract

4 cups confectioners' sugar

4 ounces (115g) whipped frozen topping (about ½× 8-ounce/225g container), thawed (optional)

Sprinkles, chocolate syrup, and crumbled Heath Toffee Bars, for garnish (optional)

Special equipment

Stand mixer with a paddle attachment

9×13-inch (23×33cm) baking dish

1. Preheat the oven to 350°F (180°C). Line a 9×13-inch (23×33cm) baking dish with parchment paper and lightly grease with cooking spray or butter.

2. In the bowl of a stand mixer fitted with the paddle attachment, beat the butter, granulated sugar, and vegetable oil on medium for about 2 or 3 minutes. Slowly incorporate the eggs, one at a time, and beat until fully combined.

3. In a separate bowl, add the all-purpose flour, baking powder, baking soda, cocoa powder, and salt.

4. Measure the buttermilk in a liquid measuring cup and add the vanilla extract.

5. With the mixer on low, add the dry ingredients to the wet ingredients, 1/3 at a time, alternating with the vanilla milk until everything is incorporated. Scrape down the bowl using a rubber spatula as needed.

6. Pour the batter into the prepared baking dish, and bake on the middle oven rack for 35 to 40 minutes. Check using the handy toothpick trick—stick it in the center of the cake; if it comes out clean, the cake is done. Remove the cake from the oven, and let it sit in the baking dish for at least 20 to 30 minutes or until cooled.

7. Carefully remove the cake from the baking dish. Cut it into three sections to make a three-tier square cake, or cut it horizontally so you'll have two sheets of cake.

8. While the cake bakes, make the frosting. In the bowl of a stand mixer fitted with the paddle attachment, whip the cream cheese, if using, butter, caramel sauce, if using, vanilla extract, and confectioners' sugar until it's light and fluffy. Using a spatula, fold in the whipped topping, if using, so it's incredibly light and fluffy.

9. If you cut two cake layers, add half of the frosting to the top cake layer, and spread it evenly. Add half of the caramel sauce, some chocolate syrup, sprinkles, and crumbled Heath bar, if using, to the top of the bottom cake layer. Add the top cake layer, and frost it, repeating the process. Garnish with the remaining sprinkles, caramel, chocolate syrup, and Heath bar, and serve. (If you cut three cake layers, use a third of the frosting and garnishes per layer.) Store the cake in an air-tight container in the fridge for up to one week.

INDEX

INDEX

ACKNOWLEDGMENTS

I want to thank everyone who had their hand in this cookie jar of a book.

I want to thank you, reader, for asking for this book. Thank you for taking the time to read it, for joining me in this random but curated collection of recipes I love, and for listening to my stories. Thank you for trying fun and interesting foods and for sharing your love and love for cooking. I'm extremely thankful for each and every one of you. You helped me choose to take the good parts of my life as well as the hardships and inspire others to cook and love one another! I'm thankful for everyone who has helped me get to this point, and I want to tell the people who can relate to my experiences, I see you. You can never appreciate a mountain if you haven't been in a valley, so welcome to my highest peak yet after being in my lowest valley. I hope these recipes help create love and warmth for you and your interpersonal relationships. This is just as much for you as it is for me.

Of course this book wouldn't even exist if it weren't for all the HARD WORK, energy, creativity, time, effort, and hungry tummies of my editor, Molly Ahuja, and my team at DK/Penguin Random House. Thank you for believing in me and my vision and helping me correct all my improper grammar, run-on sentences, and rambles so I don't sound like a 2,736,773 percent idiot. This book makes me cry ugly tears, and I thank you for helping me put it in words.

To my team at CookIt Media—Molly Benton, Ronni Martin, Laurie Buckle, Megan McCarthy, and Mary Whitfield: Thank you for keeping me level-headed and focused with all my other projects!

Thank you to one of my extremely talented and amazing best friends, Tessa Hiney, for the incredible photography. You captured the pictures that were in my head!

To Molly Yeh and family: Truly, thank you for teaching me about everything in your world, for giving me the tools to create and share my own dreams and ideas, and especially for giving me a job and the time to build skills to make this my career.

Melina Moser, THANK YOUUU for helping me organize all my thoughts and create my vision! You've been an invaluable leader and friend, and I couldn't have done it without you. I'm so excited to see what's coming next!

Thank you to Chef Casey Gipson, for helping me create so many beautiful dishes and photos and for setting us up for success with the photoshoots! Your knowledge and craft show wherever you go, and I'm excited to share both on these pages!

Thank you to Hayley Lukaczyk. You amaze me. Your eye for everything is inspiring. Thank you for helping me create beautiful photos with ALL your extraordinary talents and for working me into your busy schedule. I'm thankful for all the work you put in and excited for your new journey!

Daniel Isaacson: Coming into the food world and doing an incredibly difficult job, you're a real one! THANKKKKKK YOUUUU! I appreciate you sosososososo much! Thank you, thank you!

Jane Kinney Denning: Thank you for believing in me and giving me the confidence to share my story with so many, for walking me through this expansive process, and for being a wonderful friend and colleague. I can't wait until the next one!

To my siblings, Xavier and Bella: Thank you for helping me decorate cakes and other treats and for letting me feed my uniquely delicious and sometimes awful creations to you and your friends. Thanks for helping me come up with all kinds of ideas and sinks full of dirty dishes. I wish everyone had you as a brother and a sister growing up. We'd all be so lucky.

To my dad: You taught me the power of harrrdddd...break the horse's ass...and back... work ethic and drive. Thank you for helping me build all the things that I imagine in my head, for moving all the heavy shit with me, and for always coming hungry (or hangry) and with an unbiased opinion to taste testing. Your undivided support has built a wonderful place to call home and family that we're all happy to be a part of.

To my mom: Look at all the beautiful things YOU helped me create. You share so much love with so many people without even realizing it. I cannot thank you enough for instilling in me the value of bringing people together and for teaching me all the things I would need to know to take care of myself and others, not only in the kitchen but in everyday life and relationships. Your kindness, style, beauty, and ingenuity in ALL situations have been shared by many! We love you!

To my chosen family and friends: I cannot tell you how thankful I am. I know I've said it to the point of being annoying for each and every one of you. I'm brought to tears literally every day, sometimes several times. I never thought I would ever be at a point like this, that people would want to try my cooking or share my love for gathering people together. This has profoundly changed my life. I am thankful for you. I hope I can share the abundance of love I've been given. Thank you for helping me with my book and putting up with me when I was low-key stressed or being a passive-aggressive diva. I love you. Thank you. Thank YOU for being in my photos, and thank YOU for letting me share YOU, my friends and family. YOU are who inspires me each and every day to spread kindness and love. And thank you for letting me rant about this book. I know I've said it a bunch but just once more because it's important: THANK YOU! And I love you.